THE SHAMANIC RIVER OF LIFE

A Journey into Siberian Shamanism

Shaman Ahamkara &

Sky Mother

2026

THE SHAMANIC RIVER OF LIFE
A Journey into Siberian Shamanism

Authors: Shaman Ahamkara & Sky Mother
Cover Photo: Shaman Ahamkara
Book & Cover Design: Sky Mother

Spirituality
Transformational Memoir
ISBN (Paperback): 978-90-836655-0-4

The information given in this book should not be treated as a substitute for professional medical advice; always consult a medical practitioner. Any use of information in this book is at the reader's discretion and risk. The authors cannot be held responsible for any loss, claim or damage arising out of the use, or misuse, of the suggestions made, the failure to take medical advice or for any material on third-party websites.

TABLE of CONTENTS

INTENTION 1

1 BEGINNING 3

ALTAI SHAMANISM 5

The Legend of Mountain Belukha 6

2012 7

2 THE SHAMANIC WORLD 14

THE SHAMANIC TREE 15

THE SHAMANIC MAP 16

THE SHAMANIC CIRCLE OF LIFE 18

3 THE RIVER of TRANSFORMATION: ERLIK 22

ERLIK: The Spirit of the Underworld 25

SHAMANIC BIRTH 27

SHAMANIC SIGNS 31

SHAMANIC DISEASE 35

SHAMANIC CALLING 44

SHAMANIC CLEANSING 58

Karma Cleansing 61

Cleansing the Family Karma 63

SHAMANIC REBIRTH 69

Shamanic Ritual: SOUL RETRIEVAL 70

4 THE RIVER of HEALING: UMAI _________ 74

UMAI: The Spirit of the Middle World _____________ 75

CONNECTING WITH NATURE _______________ 77

Shamanic Practices of Connecting with Nature ___ 80

SHAMANIC SELF-CARE ____________________ 83

Siberian Daily Self-Care Practice: MASSAGE of the INTERNAL ORGANS ____________________ 92

BUILDING YOUR PERSONAL POWER ___________ 97

Shamanic Ritual: CONNECTING with YOUR PERSONAL POWER ____________________ 98

SHAMANIC HEALING ____________________ 105

5 THE RIVER of GROWTH: ULGEN ________ 120

ULGEN: The Spirit of the Upper World _________ 122

CONNECTING WITH THE SKY _______________ 124

Shamanic Ritual: THE TREE of WISHES _______ 127

SHAMANIC TRAINING ____________________ 135

FULFILLING YOUR DESTINY & ______________ 150

SHARING SHAMANIC WISDOM ______________ 150

THE SPIRIT of SIBERIA ____________________ 158

The Legend of Altai ____________________ 159

The Call of Mount Belukha ________________ 161

SHAMANIC NAME ______________________ 170

6 THE ETERNAL RIVER: TENGRI ________ 176

TENGRI: The Spirit of the Universe ____________ 177

CONSCIOUS LIVING & DREAMING ___________ 179

CONNECTING WITH THE OCEAN OF TENGRI___ 181

Shamanic Ritual: QUESTION TO TENGRI _____ 188

SHAMANIC DEATH_________________________ 192

Shamanic Death Ritual: THE SIBERIAN SWEAT LODGE CEREMONY 'CHADIR'_____________ 193

7 CONCLUDING________________________ 202

Shamanic Life Rules ________________________ 210

GRATITUDE __________________________ 211

WISH _______________________________ 212

ABOUT US____________________________ 213

INTENTION

Those who seek, shall find. In our age where travelling across cities, countries, and continents is easier than ever before, spiritual seekers are often attracted to the "exotic", to the wisdom from faraway lands and peoples. There is a diversity of shamanic mythology, traditions, and rituals passed on from elders from all around the world. Yet the core of shamanic wisdom is universal.

Shamanism teaches us that we actually do not need to seek far. It is the rhythms of nature, the life we live, and the spirits all around us that offer us the most valuable lessons and knowledge. Whether you use shamanic wisdom to live more consciously or to become a spiritual practitioner, a healer, or a teacher, it is essential to choose your own path and to walk this path with dedication.

If you are holding this book in your hands, *your path* has led you to **Siberian shamanism**, to the lands of **Siberia**. And to the beautiful **Altai**, the sacred lands we will share the legends and wisdom of in this book.

Siberia, where the home of shamanism lies, fed by a myriad of local cultures, peoples, beliefs, and rituals. Siberia, where the heart of Asia beats, where the endless steppes meet the rivers and the mountains. Siberia, where the rhythms and spirits of nature are woven into daily life, from the snowflakes to the birch trees. Siberia, where the footsteps and the wisdom of shamans have survived millions of human lives.

Does the shamanic path find the shaman, or does the shaman find the shamanic path? Maybe you were *born* to walk the shamanic path. Maybe you are *choosing* to walk the shamanic path. Come walk with us, as we introduce you to the world of shamans through real life stories, through our ***shamanic rivers of life***. Let us take you on a journey, through the world of spirits, through Siberian shamanism, as a calling and as a way of life. May this calling and the wisdom of the ancients light your path.

1

BEGINNING

Let us begin with the word **shaman**. The word shaman originates from the verb '*sa*': to know. This is why a shaman is often called a 'seer', a 'knower'.

In the modern world, shamans are social figures, establishing the connection between the world of material reality and the world of spirits. Shamans are considered as natural healers who have taken up the task of helping those who suffer from physical or moral problems.

Shamans practice their activities in a certain 'shamanic state of consciousness', the so-called **trance**. This is necessary for the contact with the world of spirits, the unseen world. By entering an altered state of consciousness, shamans contact their spirit guides and helpers to determine how to help a person.

A shaman knows that everything that exists has a soul and is alive, so by changing the state of their consciousness, they are able to come into contact with spirits, soul, and power. Through this communication, a shaman learns and receives help from spirits.

According to archaeological and ethnological research, we can confidently conclude that shamanic methods are at least 20,000 years old. Some even argue that shamanic practices have existed possibly even for 200,000 years all over the world, including in Europe.

Nowadays, shamanic knowledge continues to live mainly among peoples whose culture is considered as "primitive". The knowledge these cultures maintain has been acquired through the efforts of hundreds of generations of people constantly balancing on the edge of life and death. For the ancestors of these people, shamanism was virtually the only means of coping with disease and other dangers of a hostile environment. Almost none of these cultures have left behind written records, and for this reason, the descendants of these people who continue to keep the ancient knowledge in their memory, are very valuable to us. We can only learn the subtleties of shamanic practices from the surviving representatives of these peoples.

The most remarkable aspect of shamanic methods is that they are almost the same in every corner of the world. In Siberia and Central Asia, in North and South America, in Australia and South Africa, in Eastern and Northern Europe – overall, we see remarkable similarities in the methods used. The reason for this, of course, is not the lack of imagination of the "primitive" peoples. There is a great difference in the structure of their societies, art, economics, and many other facets of their cultures. Nevertheless, shamanic knowledge has operated in the same way for thousands of years, passing through all the tests of time, place, and misconceptions; and people in completely different cultures, independently of each other, came to the same conclusions, to the same principles and methods of healing and achieving shamanic power.

Shamanism is the oldest spiritual tradition on Earth. It appeared much earlier than many spiritual teachings as it is based on nature and its manifestations, forces that were identified with gods and spirits. Shamanism is not a religion, but a way of communicating with higher entities and beings of another plane. Shamans work as intermediaries between the human world and the spirit world. What distinguishes shamans from other healers is the ability to go into trance, to interact with spirits, and to see what is inaccessible to others.

ALTAI SHAMANISM

In the Altai, shamans are called as ***kam***. It is believed that they have an inherited gift to treat people with rituals. Shamans pass trials and tribulations under the patronage of spirits and under the supervision of experienced shamans. When a kam receives their drum, they are recognized as the chosen one of the gods. A shaman serves as a guide between the human world and the world of nature. People come to the kams for healing from physical and mental suffering.

In different cultures, the definition of who can become a shaman varies. The main methods are considered to be the inheritance of the shamanic profession and the summoning of spirits. Among the Altai people in Siberia, you can actually *choose* to become a shaman. If you choose this path, sooner or later, the sacred mountain of Belukha calls you.

The Legend of Mountain Belukha

In the center of Siberia stands the sacred **Belukha Mountain** – the highest mountain in Siberia. Belukha is considered to be an energy bridge offering a connection to the world of the gods. Altaians believe that the Goddess Umai, who is the highest deity among the Turkic peoples and the personification of the feminine principle and creative power, lives on the top of Belukha.

Near Mountain Belukha, everything is saturated with light, energy, and strength. Locals say that the mountain has healing power: The people who go there have their diseases receding, and their well-being improves.

Altai people see Mount Belukha as sacred and mystical. It is believed that when the times of global wars, floods, and earthquakes hit the Earth, a woman will come out of the mountain to stop all these disasters. The end of the world will only come if the peaks of Belukha are destroyed and fall to the ground.

In 1900, one of the peaks of Belukha changed its contour, and in 1904 the second peak changed. The local expectation that the end of the world was near, as predicted by the legend, became stronger.

And in 2012, the terrain in the Delone area and towards Belukha began to change its shape quite intensively. Some seemingly immovable glaciers split and crumbled.

2012

Matters of life and death, of beginnings and endings, have fascinated human-beings since time immemorial. Even if 2012 did not mark the end of the world, something has definitely shifted that year.

As we continue to navigate the current times of chaos, uncertainty, change, and transformation, the search for meaning and guidance is only rising. In this pursuit for meaning, spiritual teachers provide their guidance, while students seek and find guidance in their teachings.

In the notorious year of 2012, some of us were already walking their shamanic path, and some were about to explore their shamanic calling and to start walking their own paths. We were all in the flow of our own rivers.

JANUARY 2012,
Yekaterinburg (RUS[1])

Ahamkara is ready for the change of times. According to the Siberian calendar, the end of the Fox Time[2] has arrived. The time of lies and manipulation, of material attachment is ending. The dark times are closing.

---

[1] Russia

[2] Between the years 392-2012

The night will now give its way to the morning. The dawn is near. The Wolf Time[3] is about to begin. The time of honesty, freedom, and responsibility, the time of releasing attachments is coming. The light is about to shine.

As a shaman, Ahamkara is looking forward to the Time of the Wolf. This new era speaks to his personality and way of being. And he knows that the world will need more shamans and more shamanic wisdom than ever before. He is ready and determined to contribute to this historical evolution, to walk firmer on his shamanic path, and to fulfill his destiny further.

DECEMBER 2012,
Smilde (NL[4])

Mura is looking back to a whole year that has been a turning point in her life. 2012 began with the big decision of selling their house and looking for a new place where they can both live and set up the spiritual center they have been dreaming of. After searching and asking around for a suitable location for some time, they receive a tip from an acquaintance that a reformed church with a family house next to it is available in Smilde.

This marks the beginning of the trajectory towards a very exciting, but also a very scary step for Mura. They have to arrange a mortgage to buy this place and conduct some major renovation work to transform it according to their wishes.

---

3 Between the years 2012-3632
4 The Netherlands

Their old house is sold quite swiftly; the bank gives green light; a business plan is made, and everything is ready on the material plane. The last obstacle that remains is summoning the courage for taking this big step.

The morning before they need to finalize their decision, Mura has a moment of contemplation under the shower. 'What do I want to tell my grandchildren later?', she thinks:

> We had a chance to buy a church and build a spiritual center, but we were too scared do it and took the safe option.
>
> <u>OR</u>
>
> We took a chance, bought a church and started our spiritual center. It did not work out in the end, but we learned a lot.

And so she comes to the realization that even the worst case scenario is better than not taking this step. They sign the mortgage contract, paving the way to the birth of their spiritual center, Centrum Lumos.

To mark this significant beginning in their life, they organize an end of the year celebration with their circle of friends and visitors of their spiritual center. With this New Year Celebration, they want to strengthen the family feeling which they are aiming to create with their center. As the new caretakers of this church, they embrace equality as their basic philosophy: The church will become a place where everyone is welcome, and where the teacher can be a student and the student a teacher.

Mura welcomes everyone on the evening of 31 December 2012. She is proud of the trust and courage they have had in this journey, thanks to which they are all gathered in their spiritual center that night. She feels that her life will change now that she has allowed more abundance and expansion into her life.

With a joyful spiritual evening filled with meditation, art, play, and dance, they welcome the new year. At 00:00, they let go of the old year with the light balloons they release into the sky. With a fulfilled heart, Mura welcomes 2013. She is looking forward to another big dream that is about to come true for her – her trip to Siberia, to the Altai. She will finally answer the call of Mount Belukha.

DECEMBER 2012,
Assen (NL)

Germaine's father had a stroke in 2008 and is partially paralyzed. His situation has been worsening, and Germaine has been taking care of him.

They have always had a special bond as father and daughter. It was her father that took care of Germaine's special needs as a highly sensitive child. It was Germaine who held her father's hand at moments of deep grief, told him to look at the stars, and reassured him that his grandmother still loved him.

This was the grief Germaine always felt as a sensitive child – the grief her father never managed to process, of the sudden death of his mother when he was just a 10 year-old boy. Germaine's grandmother was hit by a drunk truck-

driver and died right in front of her father's eyes. She was just 34 years old. This left a deep wound in her father's soul, a wound that kept on bleeding as long as he lived.

During these long, dark December days of 2012, Germaine is taking care of her father as a little baby, feeding him, washing him, taking him for walks, until the day he dies.

DECEMBER 2012,
Utrecht (NL)

I am packing my bags for our big trip to South America. No Blue Monday in January this year, but big fat summer travelling and discovering the southern end of the world.

The last two years have played their toll on us as a couple. After our dream wedding in 2010 followed our next dream: to welcome our first child. After two years of trying to get pregnant and no success so far, we are taking up the most common advice given to couples trying to conceive: 'Go on a holiday and relax!' We have already had our honeymoon and many holidays that have not delivered this promise, but let's find out what this holiday brings. You never know!

This trip is more than just a holiday. This is a journey, for six weeks, to the other end of the world. A period to slow down, to wind down, and to reset.

I turn my laptop on to check the timetables of our flight to Buenos Aires. I just cannot wait to get on that plane!

In the meantime, I check out the latest astrological predictions. Astrology, my favorite

topic since childhood. The magic of the stars and what they symbolize have always intrigued me. No surprises there I guess, with a Sun sign in Aquarius and Ascendant in Pisces. The fascination with the mysteries of this world were already written in the stars for me at birth.

All the astrologists agree that end of 2012 marks the beginning of a huge transformation. And there is also quite some attention to the fact that the Mayan calendar predicted the end of times in December 2012.

Could 21 December 2012 really be the end of times? 12 years have passed since 2000 without much ado, and my intuition does not seem to point to "the ending" as of yet. The August 1999 earthquake in Istanbul felt much more like it, but even in the midst of the most powerful earthquake I have ever experienced in my life, my intuition whispered that this was not the end, at least that it was *not my end.* A lot of people died in this earthquake, and my grandma said, just like she kept on saying as long as I could remember, that this was a sign of the end of times nearing.

The end of times... Will I experience it in my lifetime? I wonder... Time will tell! But now we are going to Buenos Aires, to welcome the new year in the summer season. This one is a dream come true!

And the stories continued after 2012... There are many roads to Rome they say; as there are many roads to Siberia. Some are fast and straightforward; some take dramatic twists and turns, and others are slow and winding. Each path is unique, but the common intention of those who embark on the shamanic path is to connect with divine wisdom and to heal their wounds on this river called life.

Join us now for a journey through the legends of the Altai and the spirits of Siberian shamanism. This is a journey along the shamanic paths of Shaman Ahamkara and three of his students, Mura, Germaine, and I, as we navigate the material and spiritual worlds on our rivers of life. Beware that the personal stories we share follow the logic of the spirits and not necessarily the logic of *chronos*[5].

---

[5] Personification of **time** in Greek mythology

2

THE SHAMANIC WORLD

Siberia is vast and diverse, and so is Siberian shamanism. We will need a shamanic map to guide us during our journey into Siberian shamanism. We will explain the fundaments of our story. This is quite a theoretical explanation, so bear with us before we move on to how the spirits of Siberian shamanism come to life through our real life stories.

According to Altai shamanism, spirits and deities inhabit all world spheres: the Upper, Middle, and Lower Worlds. Most of the indigenous peoples of Siberia, like many other places on Earth, believe in the existence of these three worlds in our Universe, positioned on top of one another. These concepts are actually closer in spirit to the theory of parallel dimensions than to the image of worlds literally lying on top of each other like layers of a cake.

At the heart of Siberian shamanism lies the common creation story with the **four big spirits**. The great spirit ***Tengri*** is considered to be the origin of all creation. Tengri has created two worlds: the Dream

World and Hard/Material World. He has then split himself to two parts: The first part is *Tengri*, God, the male/positive pole, representing active creation energy symbolized by the Sun. The second part is ***Umai***, Mother Earth, the female/negative pole, representing the sensitive and intuitive energy symbolized by the Moon.

Tengri sent an arrow with his bow to Umai. They had two children: ***Ulgen*** the spirit of the Upper World/the Sky and ***Erlik*** the spirit of the Underworld. Together, these four spirits form a family, and they all have their unique energy, characters, and rules. If we want to lead a good life as human-beings, it is key to understand their spirits and to follow their rules.

THE SHAMANIC TREE

The **shamanic tree**, or the world tree, is an important symbol in Altai shamanism and other shamanic traditions. It is a magnificent tree which is bigger than all other trees. The top of this tree grows high in the clouds, the roots grow very deep in the ground, and the trunk is a channel between the Earth and the Sky. The shamanic tree is a stick that connects all shamanic worlds.

The roots of the shamanic tree hold the underground: Erlik's world. The middle part is the stem of the shamanic tree: Umai's world. The upper part of the shamanic tree with the branches is connected with Ulgen's sky world. The top of the shamanic tree is Tengri's world. All worlds are thus connected with each other through the shamanic tree, which makes it a perfect image for travelling between the worlds.

Our body is also connected with the shamanic tree. Our body starting from the lower part of the belly, through to our legs and feet constitute the Erlik part, just like roots of the shamanic tree. The most protected middle/Umai part of the body, where our spine, heart, and most of our organs are located, are like the trunk of the shamanic tree. Our arms, shoulders, neck, and head relate to the Upper World of Ulgen. We receive information via the upper part of our body, through our vision, taste, smell, and sound. Tengri is located at the top of your head. This is how we can feel the energies of the spirits through our body.

THE SHAMANIC MAP

The *circle of life* led by the four big spirits of Siberian shamanism has been visualized symbolically by the **shamanic map**, which can be viewed on https://ahamkara.org/map. At the center of the shamanic map lies our soul with five different soul parts. Every soul part has a different energy and intention. Four of the soul parts are located next to the four big spirits and the fifth soul part is at the center representing the shaman.

When souls leave their nest on the shamanic tree to come to the Earth, they connect with the ***Tuss***, symbolized on the shamanic map by the fish. This is Erlik's gift to us. Tuss represents our memory, our life experience. It is like a big record with our memories in life, with all the sounds, feelings, sensations we experience during our life.

The second soul part is located close to Umai. Umai's gift to us is the ***Koet*** or the Deer. Koet represents our personal power. When we have the power to do something, we can confidently say: "Yes, I can do it!" and come into action. We can all rise to our own personal power and learn to strengthen it. Our personal power forms the foundation of our future development.

Next to Ulgen resides his gift, the ***Bos*** or the white bird. Bos represents our ability to create. Creation is a big part of our life. We are able to create good or bad things. It is important to develop this soul part, so that we can send white birds (messages) to the sky to Ulgen to create what we wish and to receive messages from the sky in the form of the materialization of our wishes.

Next to Tengri lies the gift of Tengri: the ***Ayi*** of the soul. Ayi is the eye of our soul and represents our consciousness. This eye is the *real you.* Ayi is the part of the soul that always remains with you and does not change from one life to another. The eye never dies, so the experience of your eye is very important. The eye can either be open or closed. When the eye is open, you are conscious and awake. When the eye is closed, you are unconscious and feel sleepy.

In the middle of the shamanic map, you can see the shaman and the light around them. This light represents the fifth soul that is related to your destiny for this life. The fifth soul is called the ***Sur*** or the dream body. The dream body can take any form and become any shape. Sur is connected to the moment when your soul stayed on the shamanic tree. When you are in the nest before you receive your physical body, your soul is prepared by a mother animal for this destiny. Sur is a very important part of your soul. Shamans often work with this dream body. If you feel your Sur, you can feel the destiny for which you were born in this life.

THE SHAMANIC CIRCLE OF LIFE

The ***shamanic circle of life*** or the ***reincarnation circle*** consists of two parts: the River of Life (the lower part of the wheel) and the Milky Way (the upper part of the wheel).

The **River of Life** symbolizes time in Altai shamanism. The River of Life begins in Ulgen's world, then flows through Umai's world and ends as a lake in the Erlik world. Time changes and flows like a river. It is never the same. As the saying goes: You can never swim twice in the same river.

On the River of Life, there is a boat with a human-being standing on it with a stick. The boat represents our physical body in the material world, and the human-being represents our soul. It is essential to use a paddle to steer the boat in order to be able to follow our purpose and destiny in life. We should not just follow the flow of the river, but learn to consciously paddle through the river of life. Paddling is about living consciously and intentionally and moving wisely with the flow while steering the boat. While we are steering, we need to use our intuition to lead our boat in the right direction. Most people have no paddles to manipulate their boat., which means that they do not even have enough energy to steer their life. They just float while the River of Life flows by and moves forward. If we do not steer, we end up getting carried on by the river.

The **Milky Way** is the upper part of the reincarnation circle. It represents our journey after death. After our death, our soul travels through the Milky Way to the Tengri world, and from the Tengri world, we reincarnate for a new life in a new body.

After we die, our souls must pass the bridge made of one hair – a thin bridge that we need to cross carefully in order not to lose our balance. We need consciousness to have this sense of balance and to cross this bridge. If we lose our balance and fall, we fall into the lake of Erlik, which is located at the end of the River of Life. There is a monster in this lake, and it is believed that this monster eats these unconscious lost souls. These souls stay for a while in the belly of the monster. This is a period of suffering and a form of cleansing for the soul. The cleansing serves to process the issue which the soul remained unconscious of until their death. For every soul, this is a different reason. After this cleansing, the soul eventually gets out of the belly of the monster. For these souls, it takes longer to find their way to the Milky Way.

The moment of death is the most important moment of our life. We need to prepare for this moment. Consciousness leads to an awareness that we are dying and that we need to let go of your attachments in life. If we are not aware of our death, then the soul keeps its connection to material life and becomes a lost soul. The monster is a symbol of the soul that is trying to experience a material reality but does not have a physical body to experience it. After a lost soul receives cleansing from the monster, it is free from its attachments, and it is free to go forward in the reincarnation circle.

Death is the moment of the largest transformation as it marks the time to go to the Milky Way and to make a decision about our next life. How we live our whole life is also important, but death is the most important moment because it represents the result of our life. Life is like a marathon, and how we finish is a result of all the small decisions we make along the way.

During our River of Life, we have all the five souls present together, and they help us to experience our life. When we reach the moment of death, the soul starts to separate from the body. During the first three days following death, they stay together with the dead body. After three days, the soul starts to change and begins its transformation process. The soul of the Deer comes back to the family, to the person/baby who is going to be born soon to this family. This is why we often see death and birth succeeding each other in a family.

The other souls (Ayi, White Bird, Fish, and Sur) stay together until 40 days after death. During these 40 days, the soul visits the place where they have lived. This visit is dangerous as the soul can get lost and become a lost soul. That is why in many traditions, people help the deceased to find their way to the light in the Dream World during this 40 day window. After these 40 days, all souls travel towards their own direction: the White Bird to Ulgen, the Fish to Erlik, Sur to the Dream World, and Ayi to Tengri.

Our soul (Ayi) travels via the Milky Way to the Ocean of Tengri. This is where we all come from and where we all go back to. There, where it is timeless, we can finally rest. It is calm and peaceful in this Ocean. Our soul can stay in the Ocean for a very long time, but it does not feel time there.

When the soul is ready to go to back to the Earth again, it travels through the Milky Way until it lands on to a nest, located on the shamanic tree. When a soul is in the nest, their mother animal comes to take care of them and to bring them to the other souls. We have three souls in the nest: the White Bird, Ayi, and Sur. It is only after birth that the Fish (memory) and the soul of the Deer joins the soul. This is how the circle of reincarnation evolves from one life to another.

Now that we have discovered how the **Shamanic River of Life** flows, it is time to find out how to navigate this river consciously and how the four big spirits can help and guide us in this journey.

3

THE RIVER of TRANSFORMATION: ERLIK

One of the most sacred secrets of shamans in the south of Siberia is information about the gates to the Underworld, which are believed to be located on the border between the Altai and Mongolia. According to legends, these gates are described either as an entrance to a bottomless cave or as a narrow cleft that only opens when certain spells are pronounced. A Turkic legend claims that a dead city lost in the Altai Mountains is guarded by dragons and the restless souls of dead people. Altai pagan cultists believe that the Underworld is located under the Gobi Desert – a gloomy, rocky plain, strewn with bones of fossil animals, blown all year round by merciless winds.

The elders of the Altai mountain villages, on the other hand, speak of the legend of a young hereditary shaman named Aydys. Just before the beginning of the

Great Patriotic War (1941-1945), Aydys performed a long and exhausting ritual after which the spirits showed the entrance to the forbidden world for a living person and allowed him to visit it. The young man returned to his native village a few weeks later, but he looked haggard and aged. The shocked shaman had to answer numerous questions from his villagers and told that them he had seen a lot of pain, suffering, and tears. Aydys left the village soon afterwards, went to the mountains, and began to live as a hermit in one of the caves.

Ten years before his death, he took a disciple to whom he passed on knowledge about the Underworld. The locals believe that the underground spirits choose a person to whom they trust the secrets of the Underworld. In return, the initiate must accompany the souls of the dead to hell after their death. In these old days, a shaman who received these secrets was obliged to keep this knowledge in strict secrecy. Otherwise, the soul of the shaman and the souls of all his relatives and descendants up to the tenth generation would be deprived of rest and become eternal guards of the gates to the Underworld.

Yet another legend claims that if an uninitiated person, a "mere mortal", somehow finds the entrance to the Underworld, the gates of hell will collapse causing the souls of sinners to escape from the Underworld and to fill the whole world, bringing only horror, destruction, and death.

Many Siberian legends exist on **Erlik**, the spirit of the Underworld. The Altai people associate the most terrible disasters with him. Erlik brings diseases in order to force a person to offer him their blood as sacrifice. If a person does not satisfy Erlik's wishes, he strikes them dead and takes their soul to serve him in the Underworld.

Ordinary Altaians were afraid of Erlik and rarely called him by name, more often using various epithets (such as *kara nama* – something black), while shamans treated the underground master with the greatest respect, calling him the "merciful king".

The texts of shamanic rituals depict the appearance of Erlik as an old man with an athletic appearance: His eyes and eyebrows are black as soot, his beard is bifurcated and goes down to his knees. His moustache is like fangs, curling up and tucked behind his ears. His horns are like a tree root, and his hair is curly.

According to legends, Erlik-khan lives in the Lower World in a palace of mud or in a palace of black iron with a fence. His palace stands at the confluence of nine rivers flowing with human tears, or on the shore of the sea Bai-tanis, inhabited by water monsters. A bridge of horsehair is stretched across the underground river in Erlik's world, and if any of the dead souls decide to leave his kingdom arbitrarily by stepping on the hair bridge, the bridge breaks off and falls down, and the waves carry the fugitive soul back to Erlik's palace.

ERLIK: The Spirit of the Underworld

Erlik, the son of the Father-Heaven, rules over **the Underworld**. He has power over souls, over where and when they will reincarnate in our world. Shamans usually turn to him to return souls that prematurely went to the Lower World before the death of their physical body. Apart from these exceptional cases, people enter the realm of Erlik only after death.

Erlik is the spirit of our past, our history, and our traumas. It is the spirit of death and rebirth. It helps to cleanse and brings us the energy of transformation. We see Erlik in the lowest vibrations of depression and disease. When Erlik energy is dominant, we are lost. We do not know what to do and where to go.

What Erlik actually wants is for us to follow our soul's path. It helps us by pushing us in the right direction. If we pay attention to Erlik, we can transform and rebalance our life. If we truly understand Erlik's kick, we can bring the necessary adjustments to our life and get back on the right track. Problems arise if we do not connect with the Erlik spirit and energy, and we refuse to change.

Erlik shows us the way when we lose our way or choose the wrong path. Every person has their own destiny. If we do not follow our destiny, Erlik comes to bring suffering to our life. This is a signal to us that we are off track. The signals are small and soft in the beginning but grow bigger and louder if we do not listen to them. If a person fails to react to all these signals, they can even die as a result of a disease or an accident.

According to legend, Erlik also gives people the invaluable gift of travelling to other worlds. Erlik allows tearing off the veil from the secrets of life, slightly opening the veil of the unknown. Erlik does this only when he finds it necessary and only with some mortals. The person he admits his secrets to, learns the real properties and nature of things and the order and harmony of everything visible and invisible.

For those who have received the gift of Erlik, the next step is to receive power from Erlik. Having discovered the secrets, this person learns to activate their power. Erlik assigns spirits to this person "to be instructed in the laws". They must be studied and experienced in order to serve other people.

A true shaman receives their mission in the womb, but sometimes Erlik sends his revelations when there is a need. He sends forebodings of events to people to get them ready to act in decisive moments. He then introduces some exceptional people who have "achieved self-control" to them. With the help of the spirits, he can also inspire a premonition of the course of events.

SHAMANIC BIRTH

The Nenets living on the Siberian Arctic identify a shaman on the day of their birth. Children who are born "fully clothed"[6] become shamans. Those who only have a "helmet"[7] on their heads are destined to become lesser shamans. When the shaman candidate grows up, signs of their calling begin to manifest strongly: Visions appear; they start singing in their sleep and enjoy solitude. After going through this period, the shaman candidate must contact an elder shaman for training.

Germaine is born "fully clothed". This is the first sign of her shamanic destiny from the heavens. When the time comes for the newborn check-up of baby Germaine, the experienced midwife discovers a big open wound on her wrist. During all her years of midwifery, she has never seen anything like this, and she has no idea how this can occur in the protected cocoon of the amniotic sac, which has not even teared during her birth.

Other signs follow soon: Germaine is not drinking milk for hours but is not losing weight. It is as if she is being fed by the Source.

Germaine was never an ordinary child. Her parents realized soon enough that they have a very sensitive baby in their hands: A baby that goes into trance when lifted up or when her pram shakes on

---

[6]This is called an *en caul* birth: The baby is born inside their amniotic sac which is fully intact.

[7] When a baby's head is covered with a piece of the amniotic sac.

a bumpy road. A bumpy road it has been, her life, until she discovered shamanism.

No one can truly determine if someone is going to become a great spiritual teacher or a shaman from childhood or adolescence, unless the person is raised in a community of like-minded people or is introduced to this path early on. We are no longer born into families of khans like in Siberia and Mongolia. Neither are we spotted by other shamans because we act in special ways. In that sense, it is rare nowadays to be born as a shaman, so it is often up to us to find our shamanic calling ourselves.

Once we are on our shamanic path though, we discover that there have been small signs leading us to our path all along our way. Sooner or later, we start to pay attention to the signs and begin to walk in the right direction.

To begin with, to be born as a shaman manifests itself often in early childhood, when the seeds of an interest in the world of spirits and religion are sawn. Sometimes, these seeds appear seemingly from nowhere, like in the case of the little wise Ahamkara.

Ahamkara is only three years old when he casually tells his mother that he should become a monk. His spiritual calling was rooted there in his tiny being, long before he consciously chose for it himself.

The seeds of early spirituality are often sawn when a child grows up in a religious family. This background provides an affinity with the spiritual world and the presence of invisible powers beyond the material world. These may well be the first baby steps on a shaman's spiritual path.

Germaine's father was raised in a Catholic nun and priest family. Germaine's school life begins at a Catholic primary school. Pre-school days were especially intense for her as a highly sensitive child. Sitting in a classroom and feeling all the energies around left her feeling very tired. Thankfully, the nuns let her take naps during the day, allowing her to recharge.

After primary school, Germaine wanted to go to the monastery become a nun. Her father is shocked when he hears this. She eventually goes to a regular high school, but her passion for the church remains. For her, these are the sacred places where her soul finds peace.

Mura is labeled as a dreamer with a rich imagination in her childhood. While her parents wanted nothing to do with the church, she wanted to become a nun and was very interested in God and the church as a little girl.

Mura's mother was raised by strictly Protestant parents and had developed a great aversion to church and spirituality over the years. Mura's father, on the other hand, grew up in a circus family where tarot cards and crystal balls were a part of their life. His family also practiced Spiritualism: His aunts used to make tables dance and glasses fly through the room. These

experiences eventually made him very afraid of anything that resembled occultism.

As a teenager, Mura's parents do not allow her to get herself involved with paranormal affairs and spirituality, while her interests increasingly were leading her towards that direction. She secretly reads books and listens to radio programs on paranormal phenomena.

I grew up in a religious family. My great-grandfather was an imam (an Islamic prayer leader), so prayer and religious rituals have been a daily part of life, especially in my mother's side of the family.

I never had to search for God. I grew up knowing it was everywhere, from the glass of water on our table to the vast oceans filled with millions of beautiful creatures. Looking back now, I am thankful to have received this consciousness right from the beginning.

Even as a child, I received quite a lot of knowledge about death and life after death. In that sense, I was always keenly aware of the importance of not attaching to the material world and of the existence of worlds beyond our five senses.

I also had periods in my life when I had doubts and issues with what I perceived as strict religious rules and obligations. The crux of religion for me has always been about consciously seeing, hearing, smelling, tasting, and touching the presence of God in everything.

SHAMANIC SIGNS

Shamanic calling does not just come to us. It is an important message destined for us from the spirit world. It is meant as an assistance in fulfilling our soul's destiny.

If we are not born or raised as a shaman and find this path later on in our life, how do we recognize the key **signs of a shamanic calling** in our lives?

Sign #1: Deep empathy

Children with a shamanic calling have a deeply rooted sense of empathy and a natural ability to connect with others at an uncommon level. Shaman-children are usually very sensitive and sense things beyond the norm. They may be truly disturbed by violent or hurtful scenes. Whereas something on TV or in a movie might make other children wince or be frightened for a moment, children with a shamanic calling allow such scenes to linger in their minds. They can feel exactly how it is like to be in someone else's shoes and are seriously disturbed by the pain and suffering of others. This is **deep empathy**, the ability to experience the feelings of others.

Ahamkara has always been a keen observer of his environment. He always felt the urge to listen carefully to the people around him and was curious about how they felt and reacted.

Sign #2: Clairvoyance and clairaudience

Clairvoyance is the gift of sight. It is the ability to *see* things, whether these are ulterior motives and intentions in the physical world or auras and spiritual energies. Many clairvoyants can read people's energies, *know* when someone is ill and even what part of the body or a physical organ is out of order. They can tune into other people on a psychic level. Clairvoyance often leads to dreams and visions.

Clairaudience is the ability to hear things from the spirit world or to receive auditory information from subtle dimensions. Children with clairaudience often claim to hear trees, plants, and animals talking to them. Moreover, these children are very connected to the divine, to their higher selves, or to spirit guides.

Mura is born as a highly sensitive child, but her parents do not recognize her as such. While growing up, she has always felt at home with angels and nature beings. Her parents do not really understand her, so she has to find her own way of dealing with her spiritual abilities.

When Mura saw spirits as a child, she made fantasy stories about them, so that she would not be scared She slept with her back on the wall, curled up under her blanket, even on hot summer nights. She did not dare to come out of this "bubble" she created for herself until she got married when she was 20 years old.

Sign #3: A strong connection with nature

A natural affinity with the environment, earth's inhabitants and plant species is another sure indicator that a child will become in tune with their shamanic roots at some point in their life. For those with a shamanic calling in life, a sense of **unity with nature** is a deeply emotional, mental, and spiritual experience. It is also strongly related to their deep sense of empathy.

Ahamkara does not have any shamanic lineage in his family. Yet, he is lucky to have a young mother and to experience the wisdom of his grandparents and his great-grandmothers as a child. It is these three generations of women who walk through the forests of the Ural Mountains with him. It is these wise women who teach him his first lessons on vegetables, plants, healing herbs, and mushrooms in the forest.

Nature is medicine; plants are medicine: This is the wisdom he grows up with. He helps his family in the garden and learns to work with his hands on Mother Earth.

Born and raised in the vastness of Siberia, he is surrounded by wild nature all his early childhood. Nature is deeply ingrained into his being, and he always feels an intimate connection with the spirits of nature.

Those long walks of his childhood in the endless forests of Kushva, when he used to look around in wonder and breathe in the energy of nature... He still loves the forest and the plants he

got to know as a little boy. And he continues to walk. The energy of nature is always there to feed him. The forest feeds his body and his soul. The forest is the place where he can walk for hours without even getting hungry. This is special for him as he normally really enjoys eating.

Sign #4: Age-independent wisdom

Many shamanic children are often labeled as ***wise beyond their years***. Children with strong shamanic abilities will always excel at something at a younger age. This is visible in many ways, from their intellectual and academic progress and maturity at school to their unique intuition, compassion, and empathy.

Germaine is only 12 years old when she tells her mom: "I am so old, much older than all of you." Germaine's mother is surprised, but she does her best to understand her. While the kids of her friends are busy with their looks and make-up, she has a child who is talking as if she is a wise old grandma.

"What else do you feel when these kinds of thoughts cross your mind?" her mother asks Germaine with an anxious look on her face.

"That there is no time" she replies, while her mother stares at her in silence.

SHAMANIC DISEASE

Spirits come to a shaman for the first time in childhood, adolescence, or at the border of 12-year cycles: at 24, 36, 48, etc. Outwardly, this may come into expression in the shaman losing their memory, their mind, or their ability to speak. They may speak an incomprehensible language, do strange and frightening things, or become prone to various addictions. It is often impossible to cope with this alone. Such conditions caused by spirits are called **shamanic disease**.

Spirits that come to a potential shaman can manifest themselves as people, animals, birds, or as humanoid entities with animal heads. Others do not see them and may not understand what is happening. In Soviet times, they tried to treat such people by diagnosing them with epilepsy or schizophrenia. Early death or insanity is a frequent fate of shamans who receive psychiatric treatments.

In traditional communities, shamanic illness was not treated by doctors at all but was a kind of signal for the people, an indication of a new person chosen by the spirits. Older relatives who recognized these shamanic signs invited a shaman to help this person. This shaman then summoned spirits to determine what was happening to them and to help this person embark on their new path. For example, the shaman found out the names of the ancestral spirits who came during this shamanic illness and explained what to do with this knowledge.

When spirits choose a person, they subject them to a painful illness, during which they pass a test of strength. After recovery, they are no longer the same, and they cannot refuse this gift they received by not using it. As soon as a person has accepted their destiny as a shaman, diseases and serious conditions go away, but the trials continue throughout their life. By overcoming every trial, the shaman grows spiritually and reveals their potential.

Full Moon, SEPTEMBER 2015,
Grolloo (NL)

Germaine's father has passed away in August. Since then, she has not been feeling well. It is not just grief she is feeling. She is constantly thinking about her father. It is as if he is *with her*, even *in her*, trying to talk *through her*.

Until that September night... The night that changes her whole life. It is full moon. She comes out of bed and falls down. She goes into a deep trance. She totally loses touch with the material reality. Her body is shaking, and she is constantly talking and channeling messages from the spirit world.

Her husband looks at her in despair. He does not know what to do. She is not responding to her, and she seems to be getting worse. He cannot recognize the woman he loves. He cannot reach her. He cannot help her.

Their children are panicking: "What's wrong with Mama? HELP!!!" they cry. Germaine's husband tries to contain her body by hugging her. Nothing seems to help.

He calls the ambulance for help. They come and take her with them. They say she is in a psychosis and needs to be treated at a psychiatric hospital.

This is the darkest night of Germaine's soul. They sedate her and put her to sleep. When she wakes up, she has travelled to different dimensions in her dream world. She has seen Jesus and Maria. She has even heard the voice of God. Yet, none of this does she dare to share with anyone yet.

After the end of her stay at the psychiatry ward, Germaine's sister offers to take care of her at her home. She is grateful for these six weeks of sisterly care which help her to recover and regain her strength.

Shamanic disease comes in different forms. Above all, it is an invitation to heal. The invitation repeats itself until you accept it fully. The road is filled with signs, forks, turns, and choices. Once you hear the call clearly, you start to walk the path, at your own pace.

2004,
Assen (NL)

Mura's life takes a sharp turn when she is 39 years old. Her whole life feels upside down. Her marriage is going through a difficult phase; her four kids are facing problems: Her whole world seems to be a big mess.

Yet, she knows deep down that she is the only one who can change all this. She knows she

has to process her own pain and traumas, so that she can find her peace and confidence again.

This is hard work, but the real learning starts here for her, at the school of life. The more she heals herself, physically, mentally, and spiritually, the more freedom she feels to lead the life she chooses. Her own experience becomes her motto: *Heal thyself first, before you can heal others.*

New Moon, MAY 2013,
Rotterdam (NL)

I am still full of our dream journey in South America – We have been to the other end of the world and back. It is there on the mountains and plains of Argentina that I feel the vastness and abundance of nature in my bones. It is there that I see so much beauty that I have tears running down my eyes.

And just like when we visited native Indian territories in North America back in 2008, I feel a deep connection with the native peoples of South America, especially with the spirit and traditions of the Yamana tribe in Ushuaia.

I am so touched that I start reading more about the Yamanas upon our return. I discover that this was a tribe where women used to be highly respected, where the women used to be the shamans. I fantasize of having ever lived there in this special corner of the world, at the Tierra del Fuego – The Land of Fire. Could I have been a Yamana medicine woman in a past life?

With the abundance and mysteries of South America in my heart, I return to my daily routine.

Yet, I feel deep down that something in me has shifted.

This subtle shift materializes into a huge gift: I finally get pregnant, naturally! It feels like a miracle after trying for three years, including two years of failed medical interventions. Our miracle baby is now on her/his way.

With singing hearts, we go to the 6 weeks scan to hear the heartbeat of our little hero.

Silence. No heartbeat. Disbelief. Tears. Shattered dreams.

Trying to keep up the hope. 2 weeks of praying. No miscarriage.

Next scan. No heartbeat. My baby is dead, in me.

Waiting it out, for another 4 weeks. Grieving. Not being able to let go of this baby we had been longing for, for so long.

And then, New Moon, May 2013. It is time. This is not a miscarriage but a birth. Contractions, breathing through them, bleeding, letting go. Laboring for 16 hours.

A birth. A turning point. The day after: Mother's Day. Grieving our baby's loss on Mother's Day. The realization: I am repeating history or rather *herstory*. My mother's story.

MAY 1985,
Istanbul (TR[8])

After being an only child for 8 years, I will now become a big sister. Since my mother's labor started, I have been staying over at my

[8] Türkiye

grandparents. It is always nice staying at my grandparents as my aunt is just ten years older than me and enjoys playing and chit-chatting with me. Auntie is more like a big sister to me.

We receive the news that my sister is born. After dinner, I search for a name for my baby sister with my aunt as my parents had been counting on a baby brother.

We look through calendar leaves for names that rhyme with mine. Good old Turkish tear-off calendars have name suggestions for each day: one for a boy and one for a girl. We make a list and my favorite is 'Mine', the Turkish name for the beautiful little blue forget-me-not flowers.

Those were the days, the days before the internet. If it were now, I would have probably searched on the internet to find out the symbolic meaning of this flower that was calling me and would have read: *Forget-me-nots can help you reconnect with your spiritual self and your past.*

FORGET-ME-NOT. Little did I know that evening, that the day after would bring the event that would shape the rest of my life and my family's life; that this little baby would never be forgotten.

After the search for names, I watch a film with my aunt on the black-and-white TV in the guest room. Those were the days, when you did not even need a remote control as there was no need for zapping: There was just one channel on Turkish TV and just one film to watch that evening. No other choice but a film about an autistic boy: a boy who was fixated on turning a round object, watching it swirl round and round, again and again.

I had never heard of autism before this film, and it gives me this weird feeling, as if something bad is going to happen. It is the first time I see something going terribly wrong with a small child. Until then, I did not even know this was possible. I thought you had to be old to be sick or to die.

With this movie in my mind, I go to bed. I am sleeping in my aunt's room, where I always sleep when I have a sleepover at my grandparents.

Tomorrow is the big day. I will meet my little sister. I will hug my mom and celebrate her Mother's Day. We will live happily ever after!

The day after. We wake up suddenly to the phone ringing loudly in the living room. In Türkiye, a sudden phone call is usually a sign of bad news. Just like the day when my grandma called us early in the morning to share the news that her sister's daughter had died suddenly at 35, and my mom who picked up the phone burst into tears...

It is my grandma who picks up the early morning phone this time. We stay in our bedroom. I cannot really follow the conversation, but my aunt is listening carefully, with her ears wide open. I ask her to tell me what is going on. She hushes me, so that she can hear the whole story.

And then... My aunt is in shock. She just reports the story as it is, in its nude reality and starts sobbing.

In that sunny bedroom, the home of the sweetest memories of staying over at my grandparents, I hear the worst news of my life: *My little sister is dead.* It is already too late for my grandma's plan to soften the news by saying that my sister is sick.

I freeze. I just cannot comprehend. I just know that it is still Mother's Day. I need to go to my mother to celebrate her Mother's Day.

My aunt and I will go to the hospital. We take the bus and arrive in the neighborhood of the hospital. We search for a flower shop. I choose a bouquet of purple hyacinths for my mother. *The* flower of spring. In my favorite color. One of my favorite flowers, with the strongest smell that penetrates your soul. The flower that still transports me right back to that day, to the 8-year-old girl with a bouquet of purple hyacinths, walking towards the hospital with her aunt.

As we are walking, my aunt tells me that my sister is now an angel, walking through the sweet landscapes of heaven, with the rivers of milk and honey, the trees full of fruit and gold. Heaven, the place where everything is perfect, and all your wishes come true, instantly.

I am intrigued. It is the first time I hear of heaven. I ask for more details. "You don't need to go to the toilet in heaven", says my aunt. That sounds neat!

My aunt adds that my sister went to heaven right away as she was born pure and died pure, without committing any sins. That also sounds nice sis! 'What about us? Will we ever be able to join you there?' I ponder.

We arrive at the hospital. As the door of the hospital room opens, I see my father crying. He must have been crying for long. His face is all red. I have never seen my father crying before. Never!

I walk to my mother, with my purple hyacinths. She is not crying. She seems blank, frozen. My mother is gone. My mother as I knew her. Lost in the ocean of grief... And that on Mother's Day...

I am pulled towards my father as he hugs me on the hospital bed where my mother is lying. I feel his warm tears flowing down from his cheeks to my cheeks. Safe in the arms of sweet sadness... May I stay here for some time?

No! I suddenly feel the gaze of the other guests in the room. My father's uncle and his family are there. I had already seen them as I entered the room, but I had immediately walked towards my parents.

The room now feels full with their presence. Especially the uncle's. The uncle speaks: "You need to be strong for your living child."

My father stops crying.

It is as if the world stops and begins to turn the other way around at that very second.

This is the moment that I feel for the first time: 'From now on, I am responsible for the happiness of my parents.' My father is broken; my mother is frozen; and I am the light in the house that needs to shine. The joyful thought of the 8-year-old me, the heavy weight I keep on carrying on my shoulders for years...

Definitely until exactly 28 years later, until that Mother's Day when I miscarried – the day I receive my calling, the calling to heal myself.

SHAMANIC CALLING

If shamanism has not been passed down to you through ancestors, it is still possible to become a shaman. For shamanism is a calling. The **shamanic calling** is being chosen by spirits, and anyone – *including you* – can be called to become a shaman.

The shamanic calling does not even need to come with a disease or an epiphany. A shaman is a human-being. A baby who plays, a child who goes to school, a teenager who goes out with his friends, a young adult who goes to university.

SUMMER 2000,
Yekaterinburg (RUS)

Ahamkara is studying to become a civil engineer. It is not only his textbooks he is reading. He is intrigued by the world of shamanism, so he starts researching and reading more on this fascinating topic. These are the years when spiritual teachings have a rebirth in Russia after years of Soviet secularism, during which religion and spirituality had been confined to the private space.

It is towards the end of his studies, around the age of 23 that Ahamkara attends a lecture given by the Altai Shaman Arzhan with a friend of his. From the moment he meets Shaman Arzhan, he is impressed by his wisdom and energy. This is also when he already hears the first whispers of his shamanic calling, but he needs time to answer this call.

FALL 2001,
Yekaterinburg (RUS)

Ahamkara is following the logical path for a young educated man, the path he is supposed to follow after he finishes his university education.

After he graduates from the university as a young and promising engineer, he starts to work for a military factory. As soon as he starts his new job, he is given the responsibility to lead his own team. Becoming a boss and having people work under him who are older and more experienced in the factory boosts his pride and ego as a fresh graduate.

He is earning a good income, and at that time, there is also an attractive program offered for young engineers who 'refresh the blood of the factory'. The program is designed to ensure their loyalty to the job and the company. The most significant of these incentives for young engineers is that they get a free apartment if they commit to work there for five years. This is not just a free rental apartment; they actually became the owners of that apartment.

Ahamkara receives this apartment offer. The apartment is being built, and he just has to wait one more year to live there. This huge incentive becomes in fact a huge challenge for him. If he just keeps on working for a few more years, he could quit the job, maybe even sell the apartment, and receive a serious sum of money.

Yet, even though he is at the blooming beginning of his career, deep down he is occupied by the feeling that this life is not fulfilling him. Receiving this huge offer from the company,

however, makes it very difficult for him to leave. The comfortable life he has established for himself and the generosity of the company are energetically holding him back and pulling him to stay where he is.

All these rewards are for reaping, but he is not feeling happy. He is only 24 years old, but he can already see his life unfolding in front of him: He will work at a military factory all his life; his career will proceed towards becoming the head of the department; he will own the apartment he receives from the company, go to the beach for holidays once a year, and retire in thirty years.

This prospect makes him feel like he will only be working for money and comfort. When he imagines that he will be doing this for the rest of his life though, it feels really depressing. It is as if life is challenging him and asking him to answer the question: *What is your real path?*

He is at a crossroads. He has to face his fear of change and make a choice: Does he follow his longing for a comfortable life that he has already started living or face the frightening uncertainty of a brand new life? Will he go on living the city life with a good job to provide for the family he wishes to form?

Will he walk the regular, logical path of security, or will he follow his heart, his spiritual calling? In order to grow in his spiritual path, he has to give up his life, quit his career, leave his apartment, and move to the mountain village of his shaman teacher in the Altai. He has no idea what is waiting for him there. Where will he live? What will he do? How will he earn money afterwards?

By the time Ahamkara actually receives the apartment from his company, he has already decided to quit his job and to go for the shamanic training. For him, choosing the shamanic path has not been a sudden epiphany, but rather a gradual process of contemplation. He starts to think about it, to feel into it, to talk about it with his inner circle, and to search through his options.

As he is reflecting, Shaman Arzhan says: "It is time for you to walk the shamanic path, but you can also go on living your current life. This is just an invitation for you. It is up to you to make your choice." There is no pressure, just an invitation to join his teacher's shamanic training.

The vision of his teacher is that the shamanic path may actually be his life path. This invitation makes the difference for Ahamkara. The teacher calls the student to the shamanic path, and the student's soul answers: 'I have to leave. I need to take the leap of faith and follow my heart's calling.'

The call of the shaman. The call of his teacher. The call of the Altai. This was the last push Ahamkara needed to follow his calling. And so he leaves the company and his life as he has known it behind and moves forward to the unknown.

A shamanic calling may manifest itself subtly like it did in the case of Ahamkara. There might also be **signs of a shamanic calling** scattered throughout your life path:

Sign #1: You often find it difficult to fit into a group because people do not understand you, and you cannot share your feelings and visions with them.

Shamans in most cultures were loners (often living in the outskirts of the village), and they were often seen as "different" or eccentric. Because of their unique gifts and sensitivity, shamans could never fit into typical society, as they acted as a bridge between the visible and invisible worlds. Still, they were respected for the wisdom they shared.

Sign #2: Vivid flying dreams and prophetic dreams

Have you noticed that your dreams come true? Some shamans are born with a natural ability to journey between worlds, gather information, and even see visions of future events through their dreams.

Sign #3: Frequent* déjà-vu *sensations

This is the feeling that you should be here and have already been here before, as if you are aligning with a predetermined path. These kind of experiences are not surprising, as shamans are very sensitive, and their ability to journey between worlds creates opportunities to see what will happen before it actually occurs.

Sign #4: Strong connection with nature, plants, or animals

You may feel that being in nature is the only time when you can truly be yourself. You feel at home in nature. The connection you share is not just superficial, it is very deep. You draw energy from every living creature around you.

Sign #5: You are drawn to herbs or natural healing products and instinctively know what you need to use.

Using the wisdom of the spirits, shamans can blend natural herbal remedies to heal both the energetic and physical body. Interestingly, many herbs used in traditional shamanism for healing have by now been scientifically validated. If you find yourself naturally drawn to the garden and kitchen to heal ailments with herbs, it may be a sign of a (past) connection to the world of shamanism.

Sign #6: You feel awakened, joyful, or calm when you hear the sound of a drum.

Shamans use drums to assist them in journeying to other worlds or to connect with spirits. If you have a strong passion for the sound of drums, it may be a sign that you have roots in shamanism.

Sign #7: Near-death or out-of-body experience

To become a shaman, one must undergo a 'death and rebirth' process which often manifests itself as a temporary illness or a shocking crisis. It is through overcoming and healing from this experience that future shamans renounce everything they know as truth, in pursuit of the wisdom they are destined to attain.

Sign #8: Profession related to healing arts

You might have already found your calling in a profession that helps others. You may already be working for the healing of other people or animals, whether it is in the field of medicine, psychology, or social volunteering.

If you are reading this book, many of the signs of a shamanic calling may apply to you. The last sign of a shamanic calling, however, often proves to be the most powerful sign that determines whether you will follow the shamanic path. In the end, the power of a shaman lies not only in their gifts, but in their authentic desire to help other people improve their well-being. The ability to help others will eventually depend on the strength of a person's personality and willpower.

2005,
Valthe (NL)

Mura receives her first shamanic calling during her training to become a regression therapist. On a training weekend, there is also a fire ceremony organized by an Indonesian shaman.

Up until that moment, she actually thinks that shamans are "charlatans". When she joins this fire ceremony, she suddenly has a strong *déjà-vu* sensation that this is not the first time she is attending a fire ceremony: She suddenly feels that has attended hundreds of these ceremonies in past lives. She has even been the one lighting the fire and leading the ceremony. At that moment, she feels joy and recognition, but also a deep fear inside of her.

The same year, in the summer of 2005, Mura meets Ahamkara for the first time during the Shamanic Teachings Festival in the Netherlands. It is the second time that he has come to teach there.

Ahamkara is 28 years old then. He is young, shy, and mysterious. For Mura, he is special because he is actually not that dominant and visible. She finds that the other shamans at the festival are walking around in their traditional clothes with big egos. Ahamkara, on the other hand, looks quite ordinary in his jogging pants and his spiritual t-shirt. Yet Mura senses his wisdom: 'He knows it. I do not know what he knows, but he knows it.' her inner voice says.

Mura also receives a reading from him during the festival. At that time, Ahamkara is working with a Russian translator, Olga. Mura has

prepared a series of questions for the reading which she has noted down on a small piece of paper. Olga begins by saying: "Open your heart!".At that moment, when Ahamkara opens his heart, too, it feels as if gigantic cathedral doors open in front of Mura. It is as if she finds herself in a space of all-knowingness. She manages to ask all the practical questions about her life she has prepared beforehand, but the reading leaves a lasting mark on her because she gets this special feeling that she knows everything, but knows nothing at all, both at the same time.

Our first shamanic calling is usually a memorable moment. The shamanic call is not a one-time calling though. The first shamanic call may just be a soft whisper in your ear. The call may repeat itself to get heard and turn into a scream until you finally decide to answer this calling.

2011,
Valthe (NL)

Germaine and her friend attend the first lesson of the shamanic healer training offered by Ahamkara at the spiritual center Mirre. For the first exercise, they need to connect with the spirit of the Wolf. As soon as Ahamkara begins to drum, Germaine enters into a deep trance and falls with her face down on the floor. The class is panicked and are then surprised to find her unharmed.

Germaine's first shamanic training is intense for her. During this one year training, Ahamkara

recognizes her shamanic gifts and tells her that she needs to pay attention to this calling. Germaine does not feel ready to follow this path yet. She is too occupied with her daily life of running their family café.

2015,
Assen (NL)

The shamanic calling that is too loud for Germaine to ignore occurs in September 2015.[9] Deep down, she knows that a new power has unleashed within her during this episode which has led to her stay at the psychiatry ward. It is as if she has been struck by lightning, and this is really overwhelming for her.

She remembers talking to the psychiatric nurse who was taking care of her while she was recovering. She tells her: "Your father is standing right behind you because he sees that you are so sad." When the nurse hears this message, she starts to cry: She has indeed been sad since the death of her father as she has not been able to say goodbye to him. "This is who I am. I do not want all of this, but I have to surrender to it." admits Germaine to the nurse.

Germaine is used to seeing and hearing messages from spirits. She has been assisting a medium the past ten years, and the shamanic training with Ahamkara has also opened new spiritual doors for her. Yet, Germaine is still fighting against herself, against her own power. She has a gift, a gift she has not asked for, a gift she

---

9You may (re)read the detailed story of this episode on pp. 36-37.

refuses to embrace. This is a weight that is too heavy to carry all by herself. She needs help and guidance.

After she comes out of the hospital, she turns to Ahamkara for direction. He first brings her father to the light. After she is released from her father's spirit, she finds herself faced with the task of having to heal the family karma her father had not manage to clean up during his lifetime.

Ahamkara also teaches Germaine's family how dangerous it is to touch someone in a deep trance and warns them not to touch her again if they find her in a state of deep trance.

Full Moon, MAY 2016,
Assen (NL)

Not even a year passes by, and Germaine finds herself in the middle of a deep trance again. While she is seeing very strong images of lions in Africa in the dream world, the power of the energies leads her to fall down again.

When she falls, her family is afraid that she has a stroke just like her father. They touch her to check, and history repeats itself: Germaine ends up at the psychiatric ward again.

The next morning, her nurse tells her: "You do not belong here." She knows she does not belong there, but this time around, she wants to stay at the hospital for some time, just to have a rest. She just does not want to go back to her house situated right above the café they are running. After she leaves the hospital, she is glad that can stay at her mother's home this time until she can recover from this second crisis.

With this second episode within a year, it is now obvious that living and working at a café with all the spirits that come and go with their messages from the spirit world is not working for Germaine anymore. This is saturating her gentle soul and literally making her sick. Each time she visits her general practitioner with new health issues, she leaves with empty hands as there seems to be nothing physically wrong with her. Yet her husband is still not willing to move out of this place.

When Ahamkara comes to visit her after her second stay at the psychiatric ward, he cleanses their whole house energetically and advises her now to move to another place.

This is the point when Germaine definitely realizes that she cannot go on living a "normal life" *as if* she does not have her spiritual gifts. She cannot ignore her shamanic calling anymore.

By now, she is totally lost and feels the need to start from scratch. She wants to heal. She has to follow her soul to where it is leading her: to the heart of Siberia.

The shamanic path is not always straight. Sometimes there are twists and turns along the way, obstacles on the road that seem to block progress. And sometimes you take a side path, so that you can return back to the main road with greater force and determination.

JANUARY 2009,
Istanbul (TR)

I am sitting at the office of the astrologer who is giving me a birth chart reading. "You were born for these times" she says, "You are a healer who will help people transition into the Aquarius age. Follow your heart and own your power."

With these words the first seeds of my soul searching journey are planted. I have always felt the calling to change the world somehow, but it seems that I first need to figure out *how* I can change the world. This is why I came to this astrologer for a birth chart reading in the first place: I want to get a hint about my destiny, so that I can move towards a new direction.

Once upon a time when I was young(er), I thought I could change the world through power and politics. That is why I have invested my time and precious young brain cells on studying political science and public administration for years. As the years go by, I started to lose faith in politics and in top-down solutions.

I guess this is also me growing up, shifting, softening. After I start working at a sociology department shortly after my astrological reading, I turn my academic focus from the elite (top-down) to the people (bottom-up).

I truly feel that change needs to start with the people. Only then can society change. Yet, I realize that researching and writing about societal issues is just not enough to change the world. I know I am far from healing the world as a social

scientist. But then what? Really, me, a healer? How can I possibly heal people?

AUGUST 2012,
The Hague (NL)

I am getting closer to finding my purpose in the world, one step at a time. This time around, I knock on the door of a Vedic astrologer for a birth-chart consultation. He hints that I should perhaps do something with psychology or coaching.

This advice reminds me that I had ever wanted to study psychology but did not dare to as an 18-year-old. Back then, it all seemed heavy, and I did not feel I could "carry all the problems of all the people seeking help".

When I hear this hint now though, it wakes up a part of me that is waiting to come alive. The next step is to figure out how I can reawaken this old dream. As a 35-year-old, I have no intention to go back to the university to study psychology, but I am still eager to learn. I still feel the urge to change the world, and I see hope that this can be achieved by helping individuals to transform themselves.

But to be able to help others, I first need to help myself. I first need to discover and heal my own wounds. And so my healing journey begins.

The call to help people. The call to heal people. The deepest of all callings. The calling that makes a person to want to acquire shamanic wisdom, to walk the shamanic path, and to spread the knowledge further. This, is the spirits' loudest call to walk the shamanic path. And the path starts with living and breathing the shamanic life by transforming ourselves first.

SHAMANIC CLEANSING

Holistic healing asks us to strengthen our physical, emotional, and mental well-being in order to strengthen our soul and to embark on our spiritual path. When Erlik brings suffering or disease to our life, it is a sign that we have accumulated too much stress in our life and body. We need to get rid of this "weight" through cleansing, so that we can get rid of this 'old energy' and start anew.

One of the effective methods Siberian shamanism uses for cleansing and transformation is **fasting**. Abstaining from food constitutes a big offer to Erlik and stimulates healing at multiple levels.

Physically, fasting cleanses the body by getting rid of toxins. Refraining from food activates the body's natural healing mechanisms. This detoxing process promotes the regeneration of the body and slows aging.

Fasting is moreover an effective training method for disciplining the ego. It trains us to attach less to material reality. When we fast, we start to think less about food after a while. Food also becomes more tasty than before when we break the fasting, so we become more grateful for it.

Fasting also helps_us to slow down, and by doing so the channel to receiving new spiritual insights opens up. The activities that we focus on get stronger and thus also the healings we give become more powerful.

It is key to fast consciously, whether you decide to do it yourself or whether you decide to trust your teacher's advice to start fasting. It is important not to damage yourself and your health with hardship practices like fasting.[10] You need to first raise your consciousness to be ready for these practices.

JULY 2016,
Zhivo (RUS)

Germaine knew the time to pursue her shamanic healing had come after her second stay at the psychiatric ward. Despite the worries of her family about travelling to the other end of the world, she decides to go to Siberia. She stays there for a month to cleanse and to heal. She has to make big offers to Erlik. Her physical cleansing journey begins with fifteen days of fasting. She only drinks tea, goes to the sauna, and swims in the cold waters. She releases all the accumulated old energies out of her body, so that she can start her new life path.

FALL 2024,
Luxwoude (NL)

I was used to dry fasting during Ramadan in my childhood, but it has been more than twenty years since I have not fasted. I have given the

[10] Please consult your health practitioner before you start fasting. There are health conditions and diseases (such as diabetes) that do not allow fasting.

trend of intermediate fasting a try a few years ago, but since I am a morning person, and breakfast is my favorite meal, it feels like the day starts way too late with intermediate fasting.

Ahamkara's suggested method of water fasting by not eating food and drinking water for a full day (approximately 36 hours) appeals to me much more. Following the lesson on fasting, I set the intention to fast as I remember that I enjoyed the spiritual aspect of fasting in the past.

I feel the first water fasting day quite strongly. There is probably a lot my body needs to let go of. I also appreciate the fact that water fasting makes me drink more water than usual.

The day after the water fasting feels lighter than before the fasting. Even though I wake up with a headache, but I feel less hungry than I would on a normal day after having eaten a regular breakfast. Remarkably, fasting also makes me refrain from junk food (sugar and alcohol) in the days that follow: I want to stay "clean" for a while.

After this first time of water fasting, I decide to set up a regular practice of fasting. I just need to figure out the frequency that is feasible for me.

Six weeks later, I fast for a second time. This time around, I feel the hunger only towards the end of the day. I also realize this time that the effect is more emotional than physical. I sense a new state of clarity coming up. After a day of water fasting, I am able to get to the bottom of my emotions and take up some deeper self-healing work.

Karma Cleansing

Even though the primary goal of fasting is to clean yourself by cleaning your body and your energy, fasting also tends to help the individual with **karma cleansing**: You cleanse karma by compensating for your wrongdoings through willful suffering. This should not be the intention and purpose of fasting though, but rather its result and side effect.[11]

The concept of karma in shamanism is about balancing negative energy: If you send negative energy to the world, you receive negative energy in return. With fasting, you activate the negative energy yourself and compensate for the past or the future. At an energetic level, fasting gives us suffering and discomfort. Through your suffering, you make an offer to Erlik, so that you do not need to go through other suffering in your life.

Karma is a path determined by your family, genes, personal history, and psychological traumas. Karma can be described as a predetermined series of events. These events seem to be inevitable as they haunt us time after time.

Destiny, on the other hand, is our goal or purpose in life. It is possible to find and fulfill our destiny. The ancients believed that karma is like threads that are spun by the Goddesses of Fate, and the position of these threads in the canvas of events is unchangeable. At the same time, they knew the power

[11] The same goes for losing weight – this should only be a side effect and not a goal of fasting.

of destiny to change the process of creating the web of events.

Destiny can be formed without divine intervention, but it will require you to first face and heal your past wounds and then to turn to the calling that is given to you from birth. When you are living your destiny, then you can shape the course of your life.

Destiny gives us the opportunity to free ourselves from evil fate and to overcome it by getting rid of negative genetic and emotional programming. The ability to command destiny allows you to consciously manage your life, personal growth and development, rather than just floating passively with the stream of life. Learning to shape our destiny frees us from the legacy left by breast cancer or heart disease and solves the emotional problems that made us choose the wrong partners and relationships time after time. The ability to command destiny allows us to consciously manage our life, personal growth and development, rather than being carried away by the river of life.

Karma cleansing practices help us to choose a future in which life will be fuller and healthier, without suffering from hereditary diseases and unhealed soul wounds received in childhood. The practice of spirit journeying will help to overcome the weight of the past, accumulated during the current and past lives, so that we can live the life for which we were born and fulfill our destiny.

Cleansing the Family Karma

Biologists believe that evolution is a generational process, meaning that our descendants will be healthier and smarter than we are. Scientists do not believe that evolutionary changes can occur within a generation though. According to genetics, our genes are unable to change, and we are doomed to inherit certain qualities and properties of past generations: If a person's family has a genetic predisposition to a particular disease, they will not be able to avoid this disease. This means that the predisposition, for example, to breast cancer, received by a son from his mother, is just waiting to manifest itself, and the predisposition to heart disease inherited from his father will sooner or later lead to a heart attack.

Shamans have a different understanding of evolution than biologists. Shamans know that evolution *does* occur within the boundaries of one generation, so they believe that it is possible to reprogram DNA chains and to change our genetic codes.

If we manage to change our destiny, we change our genetic code during one lifetime, and our children will inherit the new properties that we have managed to fix. By cleansing our family's karma, we can ensure energetic healing both at the physical and spiritual levels for ourselves and the generations after us.

SUMMER 2013,
Altai (RUS)

Mura suffered from a kind of asthma all her life. Her whole family had a history of lung problems. Her grandfather died of lung cancer, and her mother, herself, her daughter, and her sister all suffered from the lungs. When Mura receives her trip to Altai as a gift from her mother from the financial inheritance of her grandfather, she sets the intention to cleanse the family karma of lung diseases during this journey.

They reach the Belukha Mountain, and Mura wakes up after their first night at the first glacier of Belukha. In the early morning hours, she takes a walk on her own and performs a ceremony on her own. During this ritual, she prays for the healing of her family karma and asks for a blessing from her ancestors.

On their way back through the mountains, they visit a *banya* (a Russian sauna). After spending some time with the group in the sauna, Mura approaches Ahamkara and asks: "Could you give me an ultimate healing to clean my lungs?"

Ahamkara accepts, and they go back to the sauna for a healing. He performs a powerful healing ritual for her with the help of birch branches. Mura opens her heart and lungs fully to receive this healing.

It is a very intense healing in the midst of a hot sauna, and Ahamkara really gives it his all. Mura has never seen him working like this before. He continues until Mura asks him to stop. He goes on until he is almost exhausted himself and finally says: “Finished!” They both stumble out of the banya and throw themselves to the cold grass. It feels like they both just died.

At the end of the healing Mura is completely wrecked as she has been coughing and gagging from the depths of her lungs. It feels as if she has energetically thrown everything out of her system.

This exhausting karmic cleansing pays off: From then on, Mura never has any lung problems again, apart from an occasional cold. Her daughter’s problems also stop. The healing has cleansed this karmic health issue energetically out of her whole female family line.

FALL 2013,
Rotterdam (NL)

I start with my deeper inner healing work shortly after my miscarriage on Mother’s Day. It is now time to embark upon the emotional and spiritual soul searching work of unravelling the intergenerational trauma of my female lineage.

My miscarriage feels like a rebirth and gives me the inner power to take up the path of healing our family karma. I take up the task to heal myself and my family. I decide that the story of infertility and loss will stop with me: a history of miscarriages, of babies and children who died too soon, and of mothers carrying this grief in their hearts.

I let the fact sink in that my great-grandmother has given birth 11 times and has lost 7 of her babies. I realize that I am the granddaughter of her last daughter, born out of her last pregnancy. I feel so much respect for this strong woman who could open her body and heart to yet another pregnancy after experiencing so many losses. If it was not for her, my grandmother, my mother, and I would never be born.

If I had not miscarried on the exact day my sister died 28 years ago, I would have never thought that generations of loss would manifest themselves in my miscarriages and failure to conceive. After years of trying and searching, I finally receive the clearest sign from the universe that brings me the key to my healing.

DECEMBER 2013,
Rotterdam (NL)

My healing path leads me to systemic work and family constellations, one of the valuable methods that help unravel hidden family stories and honor lost children whose stories have only been told behind closed doors.

I find a family constellation evening nearby and invite my friend Diana from my writing course to join. I have recently written a poem on the loss of my sister, and Diana has been touched by this story. When the facilitator of the constellation asks for someone to represent my sister, Diana volunteers for the task.

Finally, I can tell my sister how much I have missed her. Finally, my sister can be seen. It dawns on me that my sister does not even have a grave or tombstone of her own. Back in the days, babies who died so soon after birth were not even officially registered. It is as if they have never existed, never lived. I realize that it is quite a big step to start talking about her openly and to own her as my sister. I am not an only child after all...

The constellation also reveals that I have taken up the weight of this loss. I find it hard after carrying it for so many years, but I manage to symbolically hand over this weight to my parents.

MAY 2014,
Delft (NL)

As long as I know myself, I have had vivid dreams. Lately, I have been seeing a recurrent dream of being pregnant and even of giving birth, but that this baby is not mine. It is my mother's!

By now, we are receiving our second IVF treatment after the failure of the first IVF. While we are beginning to lose faith, this dream is a new invitation from my unconscious to work further on cleansing my family karma.

I find a regression therapist, Wendy, who is also specialized in dream analysis. It is only after I talk about this dream with her that this recurrent dream stops, as if it was waiting to be seen and waiting to be shared.

With Wendy, we go deep: We regress back to my own birth, and we talk about the losses of all the women in my family. I feel it in my bones that working on these traumas brings me closer to healing, closer to our baby we have been longing for, for so long.

Spring 2024,
PERU

Germaine's uncle was a missionary in Peru. He used to visit them once every five years and bring gifts from the natives he was teaching. He had very old Bibles, and her mother gives her these old Bibles when he dies. When she receives these Bibles, she knows that she needs to go to Peru herself.

Germaine has a magical journey through Peru with her daughter. She visits all the places where her uncle has worked. This gives her the chance to cleanse karma of past lives and to receive this energy. She also receives an initiation from a past life in Peru during her dream one night.

When she returns from Peru, she knows that she now wants to divorce from her husband. The relationship with her husband is still good, but it has become more of a friendship. She realizes she has to finally let go of this chapter of her life.

Within a few weeks she buys a new flat in Assen. Everything seems to move towards closure. A lot is transforming, and the spirits are helping her throughout this process. She also receives Ahamkara's support. It is a big step for her to divorce, even though she has also considered this option in the past.

During this period, she also has a vision of a rope around her neck in Grolloo. She realizes that this happened during a past life of hers in Grolloo, and this was probably why she had never felt good to live there.

When the divorce has been finalized, she has a vision of a black Apache tear and a prison. The

tear turns into gold, and the prison door opens. For her, this is a sign that she is finally free after her divorce. It was a karmic cycle that came to a close.

Shortly after, she hears the sound and sees the image of the lid of the well of karma closing on her back. Her past is now behind her, and she does not need to carry the weight of it on her back anymore. This is a confirmation from the spirits that she has healed her karmic wounds and can make a fresh start.

SHAMANIC REBIRTH

On this journey called the River of Life, sooner or later, we go through experiences that weigh heavy on our soul. There are shamanic ways of healing these traumatic events. One shamanic method that has become widely known is *revisiting past events*, which helps to strip memories of their emotional charge and to forgive ourselves and others.

Another major method of shamanic healing is to summon up the personal power that belongs to us. Every person is given the power to live a fulfilling life at birth. Negative experiences may lead us to lose our personal power if our energy is directed towards this past trauma.

Traumatic life events bring suffering and discomfort. During these dramatic times of suffering that feel like death, we may lose parts of our soul. It is as if a piece of our soul is so wounded that it stays behind, stuck in time, in the Underworld of Erlik, while our life continues to move forward. When we become conscious of this lost soul part, we search for wholeness, for the unwounded person we ever were before this painful life event took place.

Ancient shamanic practices of journeying heal these wounds of the soul by getting rid of such burdens from the past. With the ritual of **Soul Retrieval**, we search for this lost part of the soul to bring it back to our soul, so that we can regain our personal power. A soul retrieval ritual can be performed as described below:

Shamanic Ritual: SOUL RETRIEVAL

First, connect with the soul. You can use a drum or a sound recording of a shamanic drum to connect with the soul and to start travelling in the dream world. When you have established this connection, you can start travelling to the world of Erlik.

Imagine a cave, with its entrance, followed by its tunnel. Walk through this tunnel, all the way down to the Underworld. Imagine that you have a drum, and you will use it to carry the lost part of the soul.

Go deeper into the tunnel and try to find the lost part of the soul. See if you recognize whether it is a part of the soul you have connected with in the beginning. Usually, the part of the soul locked in the world of Erlik appears in different ways: Sometimes it is stuck in a spider web; sometimes it is caught up in metal chains or in a metal cage. Try to see how it is locked, and try to open it. You can destroy the locks which hold this part of the soul. If you feel your power is not enough to unlock, you can invite your spirit helpers for help to open it. Sometimes a lot of energy and emotions are needed to open the locks and free this part of the soul.

When the soul part is free, you have to find a way to transport it back to the person whose soul needs healing. Usually, you put the lost part of soul on the cross of your drum, and you put your hands above it. Then, you travel back the same way through the tunnel to the opening of the cave.

Then you imagine that you bring back the recovered part of the soul to the person. You turn the drum upside down and imagine this part of the soul going down to join the body of the person. Allow some time for this part of the soul to integrate as it has been separated from the soul for some time.

In the second part of the ritual, use your drum to bring the powerful life energy of Umai to integrate this part with the soul. At first, there might a feeling of discomfort if the parts have not been totally integrated yet. When they become integrated and whole again, the person feels well and is reborn.

Once our soul is whole again, we have the power to fulfill our destiny instead of becoming a puppet of evil fate. When we have the courage to face our past traumas and to learn from to the lessons of Erlik, it is possible to fully transform and to rise again to live up to our full potential.

Ahamkara and Germaine have a special bond which becomes a close friendship over the years. Her life story is a true source of inspiration for him.

When Germaine came to him, she was in a very difficult situation. She had been treated for psychosis at the psychiatric hospital. Her relationship with her husband and children were shaken. She felt that people did not understand her; she was lonely, and she could not find the support she needed – neither within herself, nor from her loved ones. Yet, at the same time, she had not given up. Deep down, she knew that she had the right to live a happy and fulfilled life, and she believed that she could change her life.

It was quite a long journey for Germaine. It took about two years before she felt a noticeable change in her life. Two years may seem a lot, but the problems with which she was struggling with were quite serious. Not everyone can overcome these issues. Many areas of her life had been shaken, and it seemed like her whole life was tearing apart in front of her eyes.

When Germaine's healing journey led her to Siberia, she travelled to Ahamkara's Retreat Center Zhivo three times, each time for a month. They worked together every day for an hour. It was about hundred sessions in total. She did tremendous internal work to find her real self and vocation and to strengthen her self-confidence.

In the process of this long journey of finding herself, Germaine discovers things about herself that she did not like. Some of them drove her to despair. Yet each time she runs into an obstacle, she finds the strength to recognize her shadow

sides as a part of herself and her story, manages to give them a place in her soul and to move forward.

As Germaine explores her internal world with the help of shamanic practices, she realizes that her vocation is to be a healer and to help people. As soon as she discovers and starts to walk on her shamanic path, her problems begin to gradually wither, and her life begins to transform. She rises from her ashes to become a powerful shamanic healer.

As the saying goes, after the rain comes the sunshine. If we can learn from the transformative lessons of Erlik, we can enjoy the fruits of our human life. Umai awaits us with her arms wide open, to feed us, to heal us, to comfort us, to empower us.

4

THE RIVER of HEALING: UMAI

Umai is the oldest female deity honored by the Turkic peoples of the Altai. All living beings are subject to Umai. For the Turkic peoples, she represents Mother Earth, a beautiful woman who is the patroness of nature.

Trees are considered to be an ultimate expression of the power of Mother Earth. Like trees, human-beings also receive power from below, from Mother Earth through the feet and power from above, from Sky Father through the crown.

Umai is a kind spirit, the mistress of the mountains, the patroness of babies, personifying the feminine, the earthly nature, and fertility. Like many other female deities, Umai is the patroness of women in childbirth and especially of babies and small children. Traditionally, she is depicted as a woman with golden hair, protecting her wards with a bow and arrow.

There is a belief that when a sleeping baby smiles, they talk to Umai and remember the sacred language of the gods and inhabitants of the other world. Umai takes care of children until they grow up and forget the language of the gods and start to speak the language of their people.

In ancient times, a doll sewn from blue cloth was hung in honor of Umai in the front corner of the yurt as a talisman for newborns. The life and health of a child depends on Umai, as she protects them from evil forces and spirits. When children grow up, parents arrange a special ceremony for Umai in gratitude for her care.

UMAI: The Spirit of the Middle World

Umai, the spirit of the Middle World, is the spirit of our beautiful Mother Earth, of the present time and all its gifts. Umai embodies the energy of protection and the joy of all beautiful creations in the world. When Umai energy is dominant, we are healthy, grounded, and feeling in peace and harmony.

Umai connects us to the material world we are living in, to Mother Earth, to our life force and energy, to the here and now. Ask yourself one question: *Am I feeling good right now?* If the answer is yes, it means that you are connected to Umai. If you do not feel good, it means that you are more connected to Erlik.

On the shamanic map[12], there are some symbols around Umai. The yurt near Umai is covered with bear skins. In the Altai tradition, the bear is believed to be the king of the forest. Umai takes care of the forest, so the forest is her kingdom. The bear is a big helper of Umai because it is the strongest animal in the forest. The bear is also a peaceful animal. Bears are often friendly to people.

The yurt of Umai has a dome, and it is one of the best places to live as its form resembles the womb. It is round and does not have any corners, so the energy inside moves around freely, and the people who live in yurts feel peace and harmony.

On the shamanic map, Umai holds a cup in her right hand and a plant in the left. The cup on Umai's right hand has soil inside. This represents richness: When you put seeds in soil, a plant or a flower grows. The plant Umai holds in her left hand represents all nature creations that belong to her kingdom. Umai's task is to protect and take care of all these creations. She helps them to grow and to flourish.

---

[12]See on https://ahamkara.org/map

CONNECTING WITH NATURE

Umai invites us to nature, to the forest, to discover and enjoy the beauty of all that lies within life and living things. The path we take in the forest is as unique as every individual. Sometimes it is smooth, sometimes ragged. While we are walking on this forest path, we sometimes need to take a break and enjoy the moment before we can continue to walk on our path again. Above all, it is vital that we keep on paying attention to the beauty and signs we encounter on our way. If we keep on listening to our intuition and guidance, the path will lead us in the right direction.

The spirits of nature are the spirits of the plants, trees, and flowers. It is essential to connect with nature spirits because many of them carry the vibrations of Umai. When we spend time in nature and are surrounded by nature spirits, we find peace, harmony, and relaxation. Being in nature is a major healing practice that reminds us of inner and outer balance.

FALL 2016,
Grolloo (NL)

Germaine returns home after her stay in Siberia and decides to stop living above their café. She starts to live in a caravan which allows her to set up a healthy daily rhythm for herself. She wakes up early in the morning and begins the day by drinking lukewarm water. She listens to music and lies down to travel in the dream world.

She has intense dreams. When she hears voices in the night, she gets out of bed and writes down everything she hears and sees. She has weekly contact with Ahamkara and talks about all the notes she has made during the week. She realizes that when she is relaxed, she is able to deal with her situation, and that the spirits help her, too.

During this period, she goes for long walks in the forest with her dogs, up to four hours every day. In these hours, she connects with the trees, with the Earth and Umai. She takes her time to ground herself. She realizes that she first needs to come back home to herself and to her own power in order to be able to use her spiritual gifts, instead of being taken over by them.

MARCH 2020,
Rotterdam (NL)

I am going out! The world is in lockdown, and people are stuck inside in their homes, locked on their screens. It is gloriously sunny spring weather outside. Everything is glowing and blossoming. What a contrast!

The Dutch government has decided to close down the parking lots to the forests and beaches, but we feel called to take walks in nature, so we take the bike or find alternative parking places nearby. What a bliss to enjoy the nature in silence! It is only us and a few dog owners who seem to dare to go walking in the forest.

It is during this period that I start to feel a strong urge to stand with my two feet on the ground. I feel I want to do this every day, but we live on the top two floors of an apartment building in a big city. I want a garden; I want trees and birds surrounding me. We need to get the hell out of the city, as soon as possible!

FALL-WINTER 2021,
Rotterdam (NL)

Our wish to move out of the city needs some time and effort. We have been looking for a house in the north of the Netherlands, where my husband comes from and where we hope to find our dream house with a garden. The housing market has been crazy though since many people have felt the urge to move out of their houses after they were forced to stay and work at home.

Since there is no moving houses in the horizon as of yet, I decide to stop postponing my shamanic path and to start my shamanic training. And with the shamanic training, my wish to be surrounded by nature grows even stronger: I want to sit in my own energy, and I want to be able to light a fire, to play my drum, and to perform my shamanic rituals freely.

And the subsequent lockdowns only make this feeling and wish grow stronger: I increasingly feel trapped in the depressive energy of the city. I want to run to the arms of Umai and connect with nature on a daily basis.

Shamanic Practices of Connecting with Nature

Are you feeling tired and seeking ways to recharge yourself? Try energizing in nature:

with the Sun: *Find a sunny place. Sit down and put your hands on your lap with your palms pointing upwards. Visualize a ray of energy entering each finger from the sun. Inhale and absorb these rays through your hands into your solar plexus. Exhale and imagine that energy of these rays spreads all over your body.*

with Water: *Get in the water. Keep your head above the surface. Inhale and imagine that the energy of water enters through the pores of your skin to your body. Exhale and imagine that this energy spreads all over your body.*

with Fire: *Light a candle. Observe its flame. Concentrate on it. It is important to feel how this healing fire burns all diseases, and that you are filled with fiery energy.*

with the Earth: *Sit on the ground. Imagine that you and the earth are one. You are calm and relaxed. Nothing can take you out of this state. You are part of the earth and its energy. When you feel this state, sit like this for 15-20 minutes.*

with Trees: *Approach a tree. Mentally ask the tree for help. Hug the tree and feel how its energy enters you and fills you with power.*

Once you start to connect with nature, you can cultivate this relationship by creating a deeper connection with nature spirits. It is important to consciously choose a spirit to make a connection with. It is the easiest to choose a tree or plant nearby, so that you can come back to connect with it any time you wish. Touch and speak with this tree. Visit the tree regularly and become friends with it.

FALL 2024-WINTER 2025,
Langezwaag (NL)

I am feeling grateful every day to be surrounded by Umai energy since we have moved to Friesland in 2023. I try to stick to my daily habit of starting the day with a walk in the forest nearby. I make a ritual out of these walks. As I enter the forest, I greet the birch trees, standing at the gates of this forest. I walk further in the forest path, stopping by to touch some of the birch trees that call me.

The more I visit the forest, the more my love for trees grow. I learn to sink in the energy of the trees. As I touch or lean on trees, I begin to notice the changes in my body and experience. I feel my heartbeat getting stronger as I touch the trunk of my favorite birch tree. I literally feel the transfer of energy to my body.

When Ahamkara introduces the idea of becoming friends with a tree during our shamanic

year training, I choose an oak tree with a forked trunk. This allows me to sit in the tree and to hug it with two arms. Our friendship begins as I start laying my head on its trunk and connect with it.

I lean on the tree with my whole spine and close my eyes. Almost immediately, I feel a swirl, and the oak tree takes me to a journey. Some days it feels like this is a journey to the depths of the universe, and some days it feels like a journey to the depths of the oak's rings. Every time, it feels like a journey to infinity in the arms of this wise old oak tree.

Some days I also get a headache after my walk in the forest. I wonder if this is a sign of a download from the tree. I have no idea. It is hard to put it into words. I just feel, and I trust the wisdom of the trees. I respect their magnificence.

And I keep on returning to the forest, to my tree, time and again. Just like with a friend, I miss my oak's presence if I skip my visits. And when I do visit, I feel welcome with open arms. I close my eyes, and we start a new journey again.

With nature and her gifts, Umai connects us to the **River of Life**. She gives us food to enjoy and to nourish our body. All that exists in Umai's world (stones, water, fire, animals, and humans) consists of *four elements*: **Fire**, **Air**, **Earth**, and **Water**.

The FIRE element represents active, powerful, and growing energy, transformation, and emotional life. The WATER element represents flexibility and calmness. Water will always find its way. The EARTH represents stability and grounded energy that goes downwards. The AIR represents lightness, creativity, freedom, and energy that goes upwards.

It is crucial to keep the balance between the four elements. Our body is a miracle of life consisting of a combination of the four elements. If we manage to keep our body's balance, it functions day and night for us, repairing itself endlessly. If these four elements are not in balance in our body, we do not feel good, and we will encounter physical problems and mental stress. Our body gives us signs and signals when we lose the balance between these four elements. The signs are first subtle. They get louder if we do not listen.

SHAMANIC SELF-CARE

Umai represents the immune system of our body. A healthy Umai energy means a healthy body working in harmony. A person with a healthy body is full of life and has the energy and will to carry out their daily tasks.

Disease and pain are signals of disharmony in the body that require our attention. Our first wake-up call often manifests itself around 'mid-life' in the form of health issues, and how we respond to this call may determine how we live the second half of our lives.

The challenge in the Western world today is that medicine is geared towards suppressing the signals our body gives. We take pills to end our discomfort and pain. They seems to help, until the body gives the next signal, followed by the next, up until we really start to listen to our body.

For long-standing chronic health issues, it may be more effective to first receive support from a healing practitioner. To stay healthy on the long-run, the best advice is to adopt healthy habits, like healthy eating and daily exercise and walks in the nature. It is also important that a healer has personal experience with practicing the health recommendations they offer. When a healer is in the position of advising remedies they have tried themselves and have benefitted from, it gives the client extra strength and motivation to follow the healer's advice.

2019,
Yekaterinburg (RUS)

Ahamkara is facing some health issues. He almost stops practicing as a healer because of them. He gets seriously overweight and faces some problems with his internal organs. This is a period when he starts to question himself: Should he be helping people if he is not healthy himself? At that point he realizes that the next task on his shamanic path is to overcome his own health problems.

This becomes Ahamkara's new challenge. He realizes he needs to change a lot in terms of his lifestyle. This becomes his primary focus. He starts jogging and working out. By adopting a healthy lifestyle, he trains his self-discipline and builds up his consciousness.

In two years, he overcomes his health problems and reaches his goal of overcoming illness and restoring his health. He regains his physical strength and his self-confidence. After his

own health journey, he feels confident to help people again.

How a healer takes care of their own health serves as an example for clients seeking help and guidance. Sometimes, a health journey leads itself to a journey of self-discovery, of healing, and of becoming a healer.

SPRING 2012,
Rotterdam (NL)

I am struggling with the fertility treatment I am receiving, and this is just the beginning of the medical process. I ovulate and have regular cycles, but the gynecologist has concluded on the basis of the initial screening that my progesterone levels are on the low side after ovulation and that clomiphene (a hormonal pill usually prescribed to women who do not ovulate) might help by "strengthening the ovulation".

As soon as I start using these pills,. I feel as if my ovaries are exploding. It literally feels as if my ovaries are balloons that will pop if they receive one more dose. IT HURTS! Is this normal? Can this be good for my ovaries?

The doubt sets in already with the first cycle of treatment. This marks the beginning of my questioning our current health system. Can pills that surpass or suppress our body ever manage to "fix" it?

The treatment does seem to work though, as I get pregnant after this painful ovulation cycle. We

are happy to finally see a positive test after more than a year of trying.

Unfortunately, at 5 weeks of pregnancy, I experience my first miscarriage. The first tears are shed. It was too good to be true I guess... Yet, the gynecologists are hopeful as the treatment has worked immediately. But the next two months with a higher dose of the hormone deliver, no positive pregnancy tests – just repeated episodes of the pain as if my ovaries are exploding.

I feel right away that this is not the way. Not my way at least. What am I doing to my ovaries for God's sake? My body and my gut feeling cries out: What hurts so much cannot be good for me.

FALL 2012,
Rotterdam (NL)

I start researching for alternative methods to boost my fertility and stumble first upon the world of Traditional Chinese Medicine (TCM). I dive right into this body of ancient wisdom accumulated over thousands of years. The more I read, the more I wish to know about the world of meridians and the connection between the body and the mind. The researcher in me urges me to go deeper and to understand how it all works.

After research follows deed: I book a session with a TCM practitioner in the Chinese neighborhood of Rotterdam. During the first meeting, the Chinese doctor asks about my menstruation, but also about my digestion, my sleep, and my diet. She checks my pulse and my tongue. She concludes that some Chinese herbs will help my digestion and menstrual flow, and that I do not need acupuncture right away.

I start a regime of weird looking, smelling, and tasting Chinese herbs. All for a good cause! I notice right away that my menstrual flow changes – no clots and a bright red flow like never before.

Unfortunately, this sacrifice to Erlik in terms of investing the money and effort in consuming these Chinese herbs does not result in a pregnancy. But I do feel better and digest better for sure – an issue the Chinese doctor checks on every time I visit her. With her broken Dutch, she becomes the first person to teach me that a healthy reproductive system requires a healthy digestive system first.

SEPTEMBER 2018,
Vielsalm (B[13])

It is early morning at our holiday home in the Belgian Ardennes. As I hold my 7-month-old daughter in my arms, her tiny feet put pressure on my upper belly. The more she bounces on that point, the more it hurts. What could this be? Something post-partum? My inner voice says: 'It is your liver.'

My liver has already given signals after my first pregnancy when I went through an "unexplained eye infection" episode, which could be linked to the liver even though the diagnostic tests did not show any liver abnormalities yet. Nice! First "unexplained infertility" then an eye infection, I thought. What is the universe trying to tell me now?

---

[13] Belgium

Then my liver had a hard time during my second pregnancy as the skin rashes I was experiencing got worse after a wrong diagnosis, followed by an antibiotic poisoning. This was by far the worst health challenge episode of my life. I was literally itching all over my bad. The itching was so unbearable that at some moments in the night I felt I wanted to die. At the same time, I knew this was a cry from my body: Stop! No more pills whatsoever!

Acupuncture eventually saves my day from this episode, but I know since then that my liver definitely needs more attention. I also feel a bit nauseous out of nowhere now and then.

I decide to ask for medical help for a diagnosis. First stop: my General Practitioner. Despite the fact that I insist it is my liver, he concludes that it is my stomach and prescribes some anti-acid pills. There is no improvement. The nausea actually gets worse.

Then a new pill prescription follows as a result of which I am nauseous the whole day. I stop right away. I also refuse to go through an endoscopy as I know deep down that my stomach is not the root cause. I stop with all the pills I am using and ask for a referral to the gastrointestinal specialist.

FEBRUARY 2021,
Rotterdam (NL)

The gastrointestinal nurse runs some blood and ultrasound tests. Not much comes up, besides for some B12 and iron deficiency. I get some diet tips to support my intestines. No word on the liver or the gallbladder. Now I know for sure that I need to search further, outside the Western medicine.

MAY 2021,
Rotterdam (NL)

I knock on the door of Chinese medicine again. Acupuncture offers some relief, but the pain in my belly is still there after a few treatments. The acupuncturist sends me home saying: "You need to work on your emotions."

JUNE 2021,
Rotterdam (NL)

There I am, back to my somatic therapist to work on my emotions. I revisit an "old chapter": my sister's death. I have been trying to organize a symbolic burial for my sister since the family constellation realization that she does not even have a tombstone. As my parents have not taken any steps towards creating a memorial, I decide to do a small ritual myself during our upcoming visit to Türkiye.

JULY 2021,
Kocaköy (TR)

I decide to paint the selenite heart I bought for my sister's grave, despite the sharp pain on my left shoulder after the argument I just had with my mother. After I finish my painting, I lie down next to the olive tree with my left shoulder on the earth.

I ask for healing from the earth while holding on to the trunk of the olive tree. For the first time in my life, I feel a strong energy flowing throughout my whole body. As I raise from the ground, I feel that the pain in my shoulder is totally gone. It feels like a miracle. Umai's healing hands come to my rescue.

MARCH 2022,
Rotterdam (NL)

The nausea and the pain in my upper belly are still there now and then, so I decide to go for a total homeopathic detox. I feel an urge to get all the remains of all the pills I have ever swallowed out of my system and out of my liver for good.

My homeopath, Cisca, is a spiritual woman herself, so when I share with her that I have now embarked on my shamanic path, she suggests that we set up a total detox plan from birth up until now to reset all the disturbances in my system energetically and to start anew. This will take a year, but I am so ready for this detox journey. No half remedies anymore; let's go!

With this detox, I experience the magic of homeopathy. With every new treatment, my body repeats past physical symptoms of my body. This allows me to go through different medical episodes of my life with a new consciousness.

This detox is also an invitation to go through the emotions attached to these ailments and to trust that my body will now heal itself as it purges the last remains. Little by little, I feel reborn. The nausea and pain slowly disappear, and my belly is happy again.

The condition of our belly is essential for our health. It all starts with our belly, the center of our body and our connection to Umai. The belly, where our life energy flows. The belly, housing all the hard-working vital organs which digest everything we consume, from food to emotions and life events.

Our belly deserves our loving attention and care. Healing with Umai energy is soft and geared towards comfort and safety. Healing methods involving soft touch and pressure, like massage, stimulate the releasing of emotional and physical blockages in the body.

Umai and our bellies require repetition and consistency. Taking care of our belly is ideally a daily habit of self-care. A moment for ourselves to check-in and connect with our body, day after day.

Siberian Daily Self-Care Practice: MASSAGE of the INTERNAL ORGANS

Massaging of the internal organs is a traditional Siberian self-care and healing method for the body and soul. The daily practice of organ massage, ideally applied once in the morning and once in the evening, leads to the prevention of chronic disease.

This gentle pressure massage focuses on the belly and our internal organs which work day and night to keep us alive and healthy. All of our organs are related to each other and influence each other. A blockage or tension in one organ is felt by the others. The digestive organs (the gallbladder, liver, pancreas, stomach, and intestines) are especially crucial for our well-being. A problem in the digestive organs, for example, may lead to issues in the reproductive organs.

Healing through organ massage goes deeper than the mere physical level. It is actually a holistic practice to connect with your body through touch and feeling. As you start practicing organ massage, you learn to connect with every internal organ and feel grateful for it.

As our organs also digest our life events and the emotions aroused by them, connecting with them also helps us to reflect upon our emotional patterns that are off balance. Have you been irritated lately? Then your gallbladder has had extra work to do. Are you overwhelmed by fear and anxiety? This might be putting extra pressure on your kidneys.

Pain or tension is a way of your organs to ask for attention and care. By putting your hands on the organ that calls for your attention, you can ask them what they need and take the necessary steps required for healing.

JANUARY 2023,
Rotterdam (NL)

I wish to learn how to heal myself and my family holistically at all levels: physically, mentally, emotionally, and energetically. Since I have found out about internal organ massage and figured that Ahamkara teaches this traditional massaging technique, adding organ massage to my skills set has become a priority on my wish list.

My professional motivation is to offer it as a form of fertility massage. I know the effect and magic of massage through my experience as a birth doula, and I would also like to offer it as a part of my fertility care.

When Ahamkara announces a new online organ massage course, I am really interested as he will teach this ancient body wisdom through self-massage. This is such a huge bonus as I can then learn this healing technique as a valuable self-care skill and test it on myself first.

As much as I wish to learn these skills as soon as possible, the timing is less than ideal: We are in the midst of the process of selling our house and moving to Friesland.

While I am doubting and weighing whether I should take up the organ massage training, I receive a message from Ahamkara announcing that

he is looking for interviewees with regard to his upcoming trainings. In exchange for answering a series of questions about his trainings and approach, participants will receive recordings of shamanic rituals guided by Ahamkara. I immediately jump on this offer and set up an interview with Ahamkara's assistant Anastasia.

What a wise young woman, Anastasia... Her name recalls me right away of the Anastasia books. After going through the questions, we also talk about the organ massage course that is about to start. She answers my core questions and reassures me that I can follow the course material at my own pace.

Anastasia then asks me a key question that keeps spiraling in my head after the call: "Why are you postponing this opportunity?" Good question, why am I postponing it really? Finances? Timing?

Maybe a talk with Ahamkara will clear my doubts. I contact Ahamkara, and as always, he offers me an invitation, much like his own shaman teacher did years ago. He says: "If you feel this is your path, go for it."

This new step on my shamanic path feels somehow so big that I am scared to take it. I decide to go for a dream travel for the answer. I get a clear "Yes!", and it is the spirit animal ant that appears.

As always, I do a quick search on this spirit animal and find: *When you are facing a chance to do something new, Ant helps you to say YES. In some instances, the Ant Spirit Animal speaks of a life-changing opportunity. At first, it may seem overwhelming, but it will bring you good fortune in the end.* This sign is definitely received!

SPRING-SUMMER 2023,
Rotterdam (NL)

I said YESSSS!!! to one of the best decisions of my life. The organ massage course has started with parasite cleaning. Just when I thought I had detoxed every cell in my body with homeopathy, I feel some old symptoms mildly resurfacing.

One thing is clear to me from the first minute: This course is teaching me the most important knowledge I have ever attained. For starters, I learn where each organ is precisely located in my body. Of course, I have seen it on pictures or model bodies during my biology classes, but to exactly know where they are and to feel them with my hands adds another dimension to this theoretical knowing.

Every lesson is so valuable. It actually feels like I am studying medicine. This is amazing as this gives me the opportunity to be a "doctor" for myself, for my family, and whoever asks for my support.

As the course progresses, I build a deep respect for all the organs of my body, working hard every single day to keep me alive and healthy. I learn to connect with them, to ask how they feel and what they need. This feels like building up a whole new relationship with my body.

And maybe the most important gift I receive is acquiring the daily habit of applying organ massage. Ahamkara's course assistant has set up an excel sheet for keeping a track of our organ massage practice. It is a scoreboard, and every week there are golden, silver, and bronze medals next to the top practitioners. I like this discipline

and impetus. It works! I do not manage to do it twice per day as Ahamkara advises, but one organ massage a day before I go to sleep becomes a steady habit.

I observe the positive changes in my digestion right away. My intestines are functioning like clockwork every morning. Surprisingly, I also observe that my menstrual cycles change from their perimenopause irregularity to their usual regularity. Ahamkara mentions during the course that menstrual cycles can even restart as a result of organ massage if the menstrual bleeding has not stopped too long ago.

Legends say that daily organ massage extends life span up to 120 years. Not sure this is actually possible outside of Siberia, but I am totally signing up for healthy aging!

Above all, I feel grateful to have established a new healthy habit which allows me to connect with my body, well-being, and emotions every day. This, after all, is where my power lies.

BUILDING YOUR PERSONAL POWER

Self-care is key in the shamanic way of living because a healthy soul needs a healthy body. Our personal power is closely connected to our health. When we are sick or have physical issues, our personal power decreases. Likewise, a healthy supports our personal power. Some people build more personal power throughout their lives, while others just spend and lose their power.

How can you increase your personal power?

Lead a healthy lifestyle by doing physical training (running, fitness, dancing) and eating healthy food.

Take responsibility. It is important to find a good balance. If you take too many responsibilities and especially if take responsibilities which you cannot fulfill, you will be tired, and your personal power will decrease. Take responsibility for the things you like, things that make you happy, like your profession or your destiny.

Connect with your Deer, the symbol of your personal power.

The shamanic soul ***Koet***, which is the Deer on the shamanic map, symbolizes our personal power and the gift we receive from Umai. Koet is also a gift to us from our family, which we receive when we are born. If our family is strong and powerful, our personal power is strong and healthy.

Shamanic Ritual: CONNECTING with YOUR PERSONAL POWER

1. *Take your drum, start drumming, and invite your Deer.*
2. *Check how your Deer looks; how healthy her/his condition is; whether s/he is strong and clean; how her/his body and fur is.*
3. *Bring your Deer to the river and clean her/him with water.*
4. *Take your Deer to the forest. Find some herbs and feed her/him.*
5. *Heal your Deer with your hands and by sending healing energy to her/him.*

Check whether you feel better after this ritual as the Deer represents your personal power. If during the ritual you see that your Deer is not in good shape, repeat this ritual again after some time.

As our Koet is a gift from our family, asking and receiving help from our ancestors is a helpful practice for restoring and reinforcing our personal power. Visiting our ancestral lands, remembering the power emanating from our ancestors allows us to access their help and support. Rituals for honoring our ancestors are powerful reminders of their presence, without which we would not have existed in the first place.

It is healing to revisit territories where we are born and where we have received our first initiation from nature. That is where our ***Ayami***, the Spirit of Nature of our lands lives. Ayami has blessed us and will offer us healing whenever we need support.

Magic happens when we immerse ourselves in our roots, in the lands where our parents, grandparents, and great grandparents have walked the forest paths, drank from the ice cold rivers, got lost in the beauty of the skies, and shed their tears.

FEBRUARY 2022,
Rotterdam (NL)

I give myself a birthday gift: two online family constellation sessions with a Turkish therapist to discover what is blocking me from reaching my destiny. I am curious if there is an emotional blockage I have inherited from my ancestors.

There is one clear theme the constellations unravel: GRIEF. Grief of lost children. Grief of lost lands. Grief of female power that has not been used at its full potential.

Now I long more than ever to visit the lands of my ancestors.

APRIL 2022,
Rotterdam (NL)

During the online shamanism for beginner's course, Ahamkara guides us through a ritual to honor our ancestors. It is so powerful to visualize generations of mothers and fathers standing behind me. All those women and men who have

transferred their genes, wisdom, and gifts to me. With tears in my eyes, I ask them for support and welcome them into my life as they all line up behind me and hold my back.

JUNE 2022,
Rotterdam (NL)

I follow the soft voice offering a guided meditation to meet our spirit helper. I am initially expecting to meet a spirit animal, but the meditation invites me to be open to any helpers, angels, or ancestors.

And there she appears: a young woman in the Ayami of my father, grandfather, and his family. There she is standing, tall and beautiful, with her two long brown braids.

She reaches out to me and hands over a small wooden box. I open the box. This is the gift she has brought for me: hairs from the tail of a black horse. Could this be the family power line I have been searching for? My great-grandfather was a cavalry, and he gave this proud title forward to our family by incorporating it in our surname.

But who is this young woman actually? I go through our family tree and find out that my great-great-grandmother from my father's side has died young, when she was merely 36 years old. No living member of my family knows why she died. How could it be that no one knows? This means that my great-grandmother has lost her mother when she was just 14-years-old. She must have talked about it. Or is this one of the deepest griefs that has remained hidden, not spoken of in public? Is this *the grief* calling for my attention?

My great-grandma had *xanthelasma*, all around her eyes. My aunt has it, and I have it, too. Ever since I have been learning about the spiritual connections of diseases, I have been searching for what these small orange spots around my eyes are telling me.

'Something that is not seen' is the answer I have often found and received. The journey to see what has not been seen, by my father's family. A journey that also started after my miscarriage in 2013. That was also when these spots first appeared, so it must somehow be connected to motherhood.

My efforts to have them removed have not helped. They have been removed twice, but they came back and actually got bigger. For the time being, I have accepted them as they are, but I keep on searching further, in the mysteries of my family.

JULY 2022,
Mavrovo (NMK[14])

We are on the road, travelling in my mother's ancestral lands in ex-Yugoslavia. I step out of the car and set foot for the first time on North Macedonian soil, the lands that my grandmother fled with her family when she was only 2 years old. I look around, to the mountains surrounding me, to the trees. I listen to the river flowing at a distance.

I lay down on the green field full with wild flowers. I smell thyme. So this is how my roots smell like, the most intense thyme ever. I breathe it

[14] North Macedonia

all in and carve it in the depths of my memory. My cells, they know this place. And now: *They remember*.

I walk towards the beech tree, a beech tree with four thick stems. I sit down, leaning with my spine on its trunk. I am humbled by this giant tree carrying me. The sun is beaming through its branches. I take a selfie of myself surrounded by this light. Afterwards, I see the orbs all around me.

As I sit there, I feel the powerful presence and embrace of my grandmothers and fathers. Without them, I would not have existed. Without my great-grandmother who kept opening her heart and womb to new babies, despite the grief of all the babies she had lost, I would not have existed.

My great-grandma, who probably cried rivers at a riverfront nearby while washing her baby's clothes. Not knowing if this baby would survive.

My great-grandma, who gave birth to my grandma, the last baby who grew in her womb. The one whom she carried as a toddler as they were fleeing their country of origin, to a country, to a future she did not know.

I feel her, at every step I take in Macedonia. I feel her strength. I feel her longing. I feel her grief and let it wash all over me.

SEPTEMBER 2022,
Rotterdam (NL)

It has been a month since we have returned from my ancestral lands, the Balkans. I am still integrating the energies I have received there.

Then I wake up one night from a vivid dream which I wish would have lasted just a little bit longer: It is her, my great-grandmother. I recognize her from one of her pictures with my grandmother. My great-grandmother calls me via Zoom (!) and tells me: "I am going to teach you how to use your voice."

NOVEMBER 2024,
Luxwoude (NL)

It is the last live call of my writing course, aptly called *Own Your Story*. It is probably no coincidence that during the first meeting, the goal that I formulated for myself for this course was 'to find my voice'.

With the first exercise, our coach Eveline prompts us to go back to an event that has changed our lives. And there again, my soul takes me back to *that day*, the day I lost my sister. With this free writing exercise, it is as if the doors of my creativity open up again. *This* is the story that I need to share with the world!

As I listen to the stories of other participants I realize how much universal female pain there is, waiting to be shared. And suddenly, my wish to share my story, my mother's story, my great-grandmother's story becomes stronger than ever.

Could it be that this is what my great-grandma meant when she appeared in my dream? Should I become the voice of her story?

Goosebumps.

Yes, I can, and I will!

JANUARY 2025,
Luxwoude (NL)

Shortly after this new insight, I contact the host of the podcast *That Fertile Feeling* Françoise to ask if I can share my story of healing intergenerational trauma. Françoise welcomes my offer, and we make an appointment to record the podcast on my daughter's birthday. I do not believe in coincidences (anymore), so I take it as a beautiful sign from spirit: She is our second child, our naturally conceived daughter. It is as if a cycle really closes and a new one opens now.

As Françoise guides me to a meditation, I feel my whole body shaking. It feels as if I am on the verge of taking a huge step on my path, the step to share my story with the broader world. I invite my grandma and great-grandma to support me in spirit during this interview. May all the words I speak today inspire and heal other women on their fertility journey, I pray.

I had prepared some notes before the recording, but as I start to share my story, I feel as if I am in a soft trance and go with the flow of whatever details want to be shared today. At the height of my story, I feel my voice slightly shaking. This story took 40 years to share – a small step for humankind, a big step for me and for all the women before me.

My story, a long fertility journey of digging deep, of exploring human health, and of discovering the connection between the body, mind, and soul and how this holistic perspective forms the first step to healing.

SHAMANIC HEALING

The key to **shamanic healing** practices is that they acknowledge the fact that psychic issues underlie health problems. Shamans know that the causes of illness appear at the spiritual level and then manifest themselves in the physical body. Likewise, if the physical body is injured, this is reflected at the spiritual level. Since shamans work with the root reasons causing disease, they are able to heal more diseases.

The reason why shamanic healing is effective is because it works on all levels – the body, mind, and spirit. If a person has problems with money, there is usually an underlying unhappiness with life. A person's lifestyle is also a reflection of how they react to their life. If they blame others for their lack of happiness, for example, this creates very heavy energy for them in return.

Shamanic healing removes the spiritual aspects of a disease by healing the underlying cause of the disease in the energy body. When the spiritual level is healed, this removes and prevents the consequences in the physical body, like diseases, disorders, and addictions.

Acceptance is central to healing any disease or problem in shamanism. If you accept your situation as it is at a given point, it is possible to find a new balance. And from this new balance, you grow and heal. If you do not accept your *dis*-ease, however, you will fight against it, and this does not help the healing process.

What you focus on, grows.
Where you give your loving attention to, heals.

Healing changes the internal rhythm of the body from imbalance to healthy. All problems with physical health or the mental state are the result of a transition from a healthy rhythm to a painful one. To solve this problem, it is sufficient to restore the diseased organ to its healthy vibration. All that a healer has to do is to recognize where the vibrations in the client's body are below normal, and to return them to a healthy level. To do this, he uses a drum, rituals, the help of spirits, massage, herbs, fasting, and other practices.

It is important to recognize, however, that a shaman is not able to raise a client's vibrations above their own. Therefore, a healer must constantly develop and raise their vibrations with the help of shamanic practices. It can happen that the shaman's vibrations are higher than the client's vibrations, and the shaman increases the client's vibrations, but not enough for the client to have visible improvements. In such cases, the client's problem turns out to be too much for the shaman, and in order to solve it, the shaman needs to raise their own vibration. The higher the shaman's vibration, the more complex problems they can help clients with.

How does a healer understand which part of their client's body has low vibrations? These vibrations are very fast, and they cannot be heard with the ears or felt with the skin. To read these vibrations, the healer uses *feeling*. **Feeling** is the ability to connect with the client's vibrations and to recognize them as healthy or unhealthy.

A healer uses the energy around their hands to read vibrations in different parts of the client's body and to recognize problem areas. The healer connects with the vibrations of the client and feels which organ in the body is sick. Then the healer turns inwards and listens to their self and recognizes exactly where the problem is and what its energy is. By connecting with problematic vibrations, the healer raises them to their own level and eliminates the cause of the disease.

It actually does not matter to a shaman what the name of a client's illness is. Doctors of conventional medicine determine the kind of disease by external signs and look at what helps *other people* recover from this disease. Shamans proceed differently: They feel where there is an imbalance of vibrations in this particular client's body and simply restore the vibrations to their normal level. Shamans do not care what kind of disease it is, how it is called, and what helps other people. Every person is unique, and what has helped one person will not necessarily help another. The shaman focuses on the individual client and returns their energy to a balanced state, as a result of which they are healed.

After a shamanic healer raises the client's vibrations, and the cause of the problem recedes, it is very important for the client to keep the vibrations at the new level. If they fail to do so, the vibrations will drop again, and the original problem will return, sometimes in another part of the body. Therefore, the shaman recommends that the client changes their lifestyle in order to increase the vibrations in general. This can be achieved through herbs, diet, physical activity, massage, or other lifestyle changes. They select recommendations for each specific case, so that it matches the energy of the particular client. Vibrations (or rhythm) and the ability to recognize them constitute the basis of shamanic healing.

Ahamkara starts giving shamanic healings after he completes the first intensive year of his shamanic training. He travels alongside with his teacher Shaman Arzhan for five years throughout Russia and Europe to help people. During these years, he is learning and healing at the same time. As he is also receiving feedback and confirmation on his healings from his teacher, this process helps him to build his self-confidence.

In the beginning, he is attached to his teacher and felt safe by operating next to him. At some point, he realizes that he had to detach from his teacher in order to move forward in his own path as a shaman.

When Ahamkara looks back to this period, one healing he performed all on his own is still

fresh in his memory. This healing was his rite of passage. He had to perform a healing for a drug addict, who was in deep trouble in his life, work, and relationships due to his drug addiction.

With such a fundamental healing, the client has to prepare beforehand for the healing ritual. He has to go through discomfort and train his body and mind mentally before he receives the healing ritual itself. In this case, this person had to stay clean of drugs for two weeks. This was the suffering, the offer to Erlik, he had to go through before the healing. By choosing to stay clean, he already committed himself to his healing.

The preparation for the healing is meant to strengthen the intention of the client to be healed. This intention combines with the intention of the healer. In this particular case, both intentions were very strong. It felt like a challenging healing, a coming of age in Ahamkara's shamanic path.

On the day of the ritual, Ahamkara first prepares the sacred space of the ritual. It is a late evening in the forest. The fire is burning in the middle. Ahamkara performs the 2 Lakes of Erlik ritual – a powerful shamanic death ritual, accompanied by intense drumming. He works with the Spirit of Addiction around his body and brings it to the 2 lakes of Erlik as an offer.

After the cleansing, the client had to demonstrate emotionally that he was ready to let the Spirit of Addition go. As the client separated from the Spirit of Addiction, he was screaming really hard. The screaming was so hard that the people around the fire were scared. As the client separated from the negative energy, he was exhausted. It was a huge release, and it was so intense that he fell on the ground afterwards.

At that point, Ahamkara moves from intense drumming to gentle drumming as his client is lying on the ground to rest. He continues with an Umai ritual to connect his client to love and joy.

This ritual gives a big boost of self-confidence to Ahamkara as a healer since drug addiction is a very serious problem. It is always a big responsibility to take for a healer. For a young healer like him, this was a moment of joy as well since he felt that he can be of service to the world and realized that he has taken a huge step in fulfilling his destiny as a shaman. The ritual proves successful, and the client is still free of drugs when they have contact again half a year later.

Many healings follow this key initiation ritual as a healer. By now, Ahamkara has established his own way of working with clients. For him, it all starts with the first contact. During the first minutes of communication with clients, when they are talking about their problems, he tunes into their energy. This helps him not only to listen to the words, but also to feel where the root cause of the problem may lie.

He uses different techniques with physical issues to clarify which organ causes the problem. To find the right treatment, he asks for hints from spirits or listens to his own intuition. It often happens that before starting the actual treatment, a client needs to go through a preparation period, for example, by cleansing the body or by drinking certain herbal infusions.

Different requests require different healing methods. To solve small problems that have just begun, one session is often enough. He advises a client to change his diet, lifestyle, or other aspects of his life. If a client follows his recommendations, they achieve good results.

For some clients, he performs a ritual of traveling to the dream world where he works with the cause of a problem. It does not really matter whether a client is next to him or a thousand miles away: In shamanism, distance does not matter since shamans work with energy.

If a problem is already old and complex, though, more sessions are needed. Solving complicated problems can take three to four weeks, sometimes even several months. He often invites such clients to his Retreat Center Zhivo. With the strong supportive energy of the surrounding Siberian nature, it is easier for the clients to change their habits, and he can perform his healing rituals every day.

A healer never knows in advance how long it will take to solve a client's problem. Healing also depends on the client: If they make an effort, the results come faster.

While working with a client, Ahamkara increases and restores the energy of the problematic organ(s). Yet, problems usually arise again after a healing because a client is stuck on his unhealthy habits. As long as they continue to do what has caused the problem, then the problem will return. That is why clients receive recommendations on what they need to change in their lives. It can be their nutrition, their way of thinking, their perception of the world, their behavior in relationships, their physical activity, or anything else that is relevant to their situation.

To ensure that the client's recovery is going well, Ahamkara accompanies them for some time after their first consultation, asking how they are doing and answering their questions. Clients usually achieve good results with this kind of follow-up treatment.

Of course, there are clients who do not follow the recommendations after the ritual, and problems return after a while. In such cases, he tries to improve the contact with the client in order to find the right approach for this person to be able to still obtain the desired results.

Sustainable healing really depends as much on the client as on the shaman. Ahamkara has also had clients who heal significantly but reach a certain point of healing where they are satisfied and do not feel the need to put much more effort. For example, he remembers a client who was paralyzed due to PLS (Primary Lateral Sclerosis) for seven years and his condition was progressively getting worse until he contacted Ahamkara.

The client got paralyzed after he saw his son, who was serving the military in Afghanistan, got attacked on TV, and they did not receive any information about his condition for a long time. This literally paralyzed his body. Eventually it became clear that his son was only injured and was being treated, but this period of uncertainty lead to the start of his paralysis, and it got worse to the point that he could not walk anymore.

Ahamkara works with him up to the point that his condition stabilizes, and he can walk again. Even though he has not healed completely, he is happy with his condition. In order to heal completely, he would have to bring more changes

to his lifestyle and fast for longer periods. When the client is not able to work further on himself, the healer has to accept this will.

When Ahamkara started practicing as a healer, he used to tune in before his 'working day'. He made a shamanic journey into the future, met there with clients with whom he had to work that day, and set himself up for a good result. Now, after many years of practice, he no longer works with such a setup, as everything turns out well without prior preparation.

Usually he works with four to five clients per day, but it sometimes happens that he receives ten people in one day. On such busy days, he gets very tired, and he needs to recover from working with clients. To recharge, he walks alone in the forest or swims in natural rivers or lakes.

Even at the end of such a tiring day, he is always filled with a very strong feeling of happiness. This happiness is more intense than he could ever get from any material acquisitions or actions. He finds it extraordinary to be able to follow his vocation every day and to turn new pages of his life with pleasure.

Many clients send letters of gratitude even months after having worked together. The best feedback to receive from anyone he has helped is to hear that the treatment or ritual he has offered has changed their life.

SEPTEMBER 2023,
Luxwoude (NL)

I complete Ahamkara's organ massage course. Shortly after the course ends, I realize that I could have received a free healing from him when I registered for the course. I am happy to discover this gift (better late than never!) and to finally have the opportunity to experience him as a healer.

As we meet for the healing, he first completes my certificate for the organ massage training. He also shares his birthday with me, which happens to be really close to mine. Another Aquarius soul, of course! What a nice surprise!

I first ask him for a healing to attract more clients to my business. He does not seem to see this as an issue to heal. He sees it more as an issue of building self-confidence. He suggests me to connect with the Spirit of the Wolf for more self-confidence and advises me to clean the energy of the house and the kitchen regularly with sage as a protection against negative energies.

I then ask him for a healing for my daughter and specifically for her thumb sucking habit she has trouble giving up. I close my eyes and relax until Ahamkara calls me back to give his advice. He suggests that my daughter connects with the Spirit of the Fox to acquire more flexibility and to receive support for releasing her habit.

The next day, magic starts to happen without me saying a word or taking any action: My daughter "spontaneously" decides to use her fox hand puppet to cover her thumb and starts receiving the help of the Fox in giving up her habit.

OCTOBER 2024,
Luxwoude (NL)

As for me, I am still occupied with attracting more clients to my practice. After following marketing courses for a year to improve my business, I feel I am still missing something. I join the online webinar of my favorite oracle card creator Colette Baron-Reid. She is giving a 3-day workshop on how to connect with the spirit of your business, so that it can guide you through your business journey.

During the first guided meditation, we are invited to meet the spirit of our business. I am moved by the fact that a tall white woman appears. I feel this is Umai. What an honor to feel that she supports my cause of supporting women during the transformative phase of getting pregnant, being pregnant, and giving birth.

What a strong sign from Umai, to bring her and her spirit back to my business! My mind goes back to when I came up with the 'Path of Umay' as a name for the program I had launched two years ago. I had dropped this branding after listening to marketing gurus as I felt this might be too abstract for an average visitor to my website.

During the second guided meditation, we are invited to go out for a dinner with the spirit of our business. The fact that the boarding room in the first meditation is located in the area I live tells me that I have a mission to fulfill in my current region. Why am I struggling to attract clients since we have moved here then? During the dinner at a local restaurant with no other people around, I ask Umai how to overcome my current challenges. She says: "You need to go to Germaine. She knows the

way around here." I make a mental note of this advice even though I am not sure yet how she can help me.

NOVEMBER 2024,
Luxwoude (NL)

Yet another failed joint business initiative, yet another huge disappointment. A rock bottom day... By now, I am old enough to know that such moments turn out to be the most powerful, transformative days. In life, we tend to only know afterwards that we have hit rock bottom for a good reason. Thank God, I am wise enough to trust that even failure is for my highest good.

The reason for this failed initiative hits quite hard nevertheless. This is because the feedback I receive from this person is a feedback I have received many times before. I feel rejected. Again. For being who I am. For saying out right what I firmly believe in.

"You need to bring it in softly" they say, time and again. Looking back to my whole life, it amazes me that I could ever believe that I could become a career diplomat. Life has shown me time and again that being tactful and diplomatic is exactly what I am not good at. Maybe, just maybe I can still learn to do that?

But at this point of my life, I actually feel I *do not* want to be diplomatic. I feel I am born to tell the truth. My truth. The truth as I see it. Even though I have gotten myself into trouble by doing this many times. I only have a few very close friends – the dear ones who can appreciate the pure, uncensored, unfiltered truth as I see it.

Where I stand right now, I also feel deep down that this is also my healing power: First I confront and shake with the truth the client needs to see and to face up front. After this is clearly on the table, then I support and guide them with a lot of care, love, and attention.

And I want more of this, not less of this! I want to go forward, towards more me. And I feel ready to receive support from Germaine to walk more firmly on this path.

DECEMBER 2024,
Assen (NL)

During the days that precede the healing with Germaine, I already experience the energies moving. My body is giving me strong signals. It is as if my heart is racing. This racing heart makes me think of my great-great-grandmother who died when she was 36-years-old: Could it be that she died of a heart attack?

The heart attacks that have caused three sudden deaths at a young age in my father's family: the greatest fear that still runs in the family, deeply ingrained in the health choices of many in the family. When I tried to connect to this heart attack piece in the family in the past, I have always wondered whether it was actually the scare of a heart attack that has killed them, as a result of which they ended up repeating the family karma...

I sink into my rushing heart. I put on some binaural beats to offer me some relief. I try to rationalize it: 'Maybe it is just perimenopause.' My heart and thyroid continue to rush. I am feeling nauseous. I guess I better go to sleep. I ask my great-great-grandmother to connect with me through my dreams tonight, to offer me a hint of what this is all about. Unfortunately, my sleep that night is way too patchy for the vivid dreams I yearn for.

I hope to receive some answers during the healing with Germaine the day after. And almost immediately after we sit down to talk, the spirit of my great-great-grandmother comes. “She did die of the heart”, says Germaine, “of all the emotions she could not express”. She tried to live a happy life with her mind, but that was not enough. And so the heart issue remained in the family, together with the suppressed emotions that longed to be felt. And so the healing begins with a bombshell!

We proceed from the table to the healing space with the massage table. The tears run down my cheeks immediately as Germaine tells me that my great-great-grandma is stroking my hair, just the way I always imagine my hair being stroked when I feel down.

Next, Germaine applies pressure on my liver. Ouch! How can it still hurt, right there exactly in the spot where my daughter used to put pressure with her little feet as a baby? I have been applying organ massage on my belly for almost two years now, and when Germaine touches me there, it hurts again, right in the heart of the pain.

“Do you have a sister?” she asks.

There we go, my sister has also joined me already. The grief of her death and what this has meant for the me and my parents... Still so deeply ingrained in my cells, after more than a decade of healing work...

Germaine keeps on massaging the painful area and telling me my little baby sister is stroking my face with her tiny hands. Cry me a river... The ocean of grief that still keeps on giving... Almost forty years and still counting. Still feeling it. Still hurting there. The little sister who will never be forgotten. My sister, a spiritual guide in my healing path for sure.

After being accompanied by these two precious souls, I am now ready to receive some healing power. Germaine puts on some shamanic drumming music on the background. She is also drumming herself and has put on her shamanic costume now.

I feel the shift in my healing journey. It feels like I am stepping up to the next level to show and give more of me, more of the shamanic me.

And this magical connection to my ancestral guides... All my ancestors I can lean on for support. Always. They are here *with me*. They are here for me. It is time for me to rise up to my personal power.

5

THE RIVER of GROWTH: ULGEN

In times immemorial, there lived a wise old shaman in the Altai. His power was immense. He knew how to ask Ulgen for wealth and abundance for the peoples of Altai. He knew what words to address Erlik with, so that he would not harm people. The shaman understood the language of birds and animals; he knew how to look into the past and to the future.

This shaman lived in a wild taiga, amongst mountain ranges. His birch-bark shelter stood alone by the river. Only those who were in great need could find their way to the shaman.

The shaman accumulated great wisdom during his long life. It was revealed to him how human-beings should live in harmony with other human-beings, the land, the waters, and the sky, with the animals and the birds, so that the Altai land would forever stand, blossom, and grow rich.

The shaman lived for many years – some say a hundred years, some say even two hundred years. When he looked into the future and saw that his time in this world was coming to an end, the shaman contemplated deeply. If he would die, this great wisdom would die with him, for he had neither a son nor a disciple.

The shaman left his dwelling and went down to the people, to the villages. He wanted to find a man with a clear mind and a bright soul to pass on his knowledge. But the longer the shaman walked, the more disappointed he became. People had become petty, and the heavenly spark had died out in them.

A young hunter wanted to understand the language of animals and birds to lure them to his shot. The smart and strong son of the Khan wondered how to ask Ulgen for good luck and wealth for himself alone. No one wanted to think about their native land.

The shaman returned to his shelter. He put on his best clothes for a ritual, recalled the main words, turned to Ulgen and asked: "What do I do now?"

For six days in a row the shaman sang and danced. On the seventh day Ulgen answered the shaman's question: "Take a smooth tree, take smooth stones, and keep your great wisdom in writing on them! Let those writings wait in the depths of Altai for a man with a clear mind and a pure soul!"

For the six following days, the old shaman lied down without strength. On the seventh day, he got up, took smooth wood and smooth stones and began to carve cherished letters onto them. No one saw his work; no one heard the knocking on the stone; no one knows where the shaman stored and hid his knowledge; and no one knows whether he had time to leave his main knowledge on how the people and the Earth should live in peace, or whether he died before he could complete his mission. Only Ulgen knows.

In the Altai, between the mountain ranges, flows the Samuralu River, where the old shaman's dwelling once stood and its name can be translated as 'hiding the book of wisdom written on wood and stone'. Maybe one day there will come a man with a clear soul and with a heavenly spark to whom the treasures of the old shaman will be revealed, and there will be eternal peace and grace on the Altai land.

ULGEN: The Spirit of the Upper World

At the head of the heavenly gods is *Ulgen*, a generous being who lives beyond the moon and the sun and above the stars of heaven. The Khakass, Altaians, and Shors believe that Ulgen is the supreme god, the head of the Upper World's spirits, and the creator of the universe.

Ulgen is depicted as a humanoid figure with a radiance emanating from his head. It is believed that his creation of the world lasted six days. Ulgen created not only the earth, the sky, the sun, the moon, the rainbow, thunder, lightning, hail, and fire, but also the first man, as well as a dog to guard him.

Many people are sure that Ulgen continues to create our world to this day, sitting in a golden palace located above all the luminaries at the highest and central point of the universe: at the top of the world mountain. The texts of Altai shamans' rites for the deity Ulgen found by ethnographers indicate that Ulgen's golden palace in the sky can only be reached by a path that lies beyond seven (or nine) barriers.

Shamans have for centuries offered blood sacrifices to Ulgen, which was usually a three-year-old white mare. The ritual was repeated after three, six, nine, or twelve years in large crowds. Together with Ulgen in the sky live the sons and daughters of Ulgen, as well as the sons of Erlik, who are the protectors of the Altai clans and are offered the same sacrifices as Ulgen.

Ulgen is opposed by Erlik, the head of the Lower World, to whom all evil spirits are subject. According to some legends, Ulgen is Erlik's brother; according to others he is Erlik's creator *or* creation. Legends claim that Ulgen actually created shamans to protect against Erlik. Ulgen is also the one who gives the gift of shamanism. He sends spirit helpers to a future shaman and indicates how the shaman's drum should look like.

Ulgen belongs to the Upper World of high vibrations. The Upper World is similar to ours but has remained unspoiled by humans, and its inhabitants still live according to the traditional laws of their ancestors. The ruler of the Upper World is Ulgen, who is also the son of Father Sky.

Sometimes, when the gates from our world to the Upper World open, people can see its radiance, which looks like rays of sunlight breaking through the clouds. Prayers spoken at such a moment are especially powerful.

To journey to the Upper World, one must know how to fly, and shamans, who decide to make the journey there, often transform themselves into birds. Other forms that a shaman can take for this purpose include a flying deer or horse.

CONNECTING WITH THE SKY

Ulgen is the big creator. With this energy, we are in flow. We feel inspired and create new things in the world. When Ulgen energy is strong, we manifest our dreams and wishes.

When people feel stressed, depressed, and lost, they tend to not know what to do and where to go. At such times, they have actually lost the connection to their future, and they do not feel where their life path should lead to next. To (re)connect with Ulgen, we need to rise up our frequency and move our energy up.

The intention of Ulgen is to create new things that manifest in physical reality. Every living creation has an intention, and these intentions rise up to the sky. Ulgen receives all of them and helps them to materialize. Sometimes we have to wait for some time until we receive what we need.

Our communication with Ulgen needs to happen consciously. Every time we think about something, it rises up to the sky as our intention. This is why it is important to practice positive thinking about yourself, your life, and other people. The more we think positively, the more you create a positive future for ourselves. It is not easy to think positively all the time, but we can focus consciously on positive thinking while we make plans for the future and send our messages to the sky. The clearer we are about our intentions, the easier it is for Ulgen to give it to us.

APRIL 2022,
Rotterdam (NL)

I experience my first shamanic wish ritual during Ahamkara's online beginner's training. While sharing this wish ritual, Ahamkara explains that the wishes you set usually materialize within a year.

I choose to visualize our future house in the countryside which we have been searching for in the past two years. May Ulgen help our wish come true!

SEPTEMBER 2022,
Rotterdam (NL)

I am reading Lorie Ladd's book *The Divine Design*.[15] It is blowing my mind and consciousness. Since I have started reading the book, I am seeing vivid dreams, more vivid than ever before, like flying through galaxies.

One night I see a number. The next night, I am offered the keys to a house with this number. *This is our house!* And the person who gives me the keys? It has been ages since I have last seen this

[15] Ladd, L. (2022) *The Divine Design: The Untold Story of the Earth's and Humanity's Evolution in Consciousness*. Lorie Ladd LLC.

person in real life. What does it mean that he is the one giving me the keys? His name means 'Godly', so I guess I should pray? For starters, I contact him via Facebook to ask how he is doing. All is well, so the premonition is not about him.

The day after: I spot a house on the Dutch real estate site, with the house number I saw in my dream. Oh my God, this *must be* our house! It is house with a deep garden, surrounded by tall trees, just like I wished for.

We book an appointment to visit the house. I am totally in love with the garden and really like the energy of the house. As I walk through the garden, I touch two of the birch trees and ask them what this house could bring to our family. One promises to bring us warmth, the other one flow. Wow! This is it! We are totally buying this house!

The deal is sealed: We are moving to Friesland! And guess when we will receive the keys? Next year in April, on the birthday of the person I saw in my dream and one year after the wish ritual with Ahamkara. What a dream come true!

NOVEMBER 2024,
Luxwoude (NL)

I am really excited that we have started to learn about Ulgen, the Spirit of the Sky, the Spirit of the Future, the spirit that makes our wishes come true. As an Aquarius person, I have always felt connected to the Future, as if I am already living with one foot in the future. The idea that there's a helping spirit that brings us to the future we dream of, sounds like a dream to me.

Ahamkara is teaching us how to connect with Ulgen consciously, so that we can make our dreams come true. Like all the big spirits, Ulgen is also embodied in nature. The birch tree, the tree of Ulgen, occupies a special place in Siberian shamanism. The birch tree helps us to receive our wishes by sending them to the sky to Ulgen. I listen to Ahamkara as he drums and leads the dream travel to the *tree of wishes*:

Shamanic Ritual: THE TREE of WISHES

Close your eyes and go to the top of a small mountain covered with a forest of birch trees. You see a lot of light and the bright green colors of the birch leaves. The sun is shining between the leaves and giving you a very positive and high frequency energy.

You see a path going up towards the top of a small mountain. This mountain is in the Altai and has wonderful views of the forest and of the River Katun. The top of the mountain does not have so many trees. There is only one big birch tree growing on the top: This birch tree is the **tree of wishes***, and it has three stems coming out from its trunk.*

To send your wishes up to the sky and to make them stronger, you have to sit in the middle of this birch tree with your back leaning on one stem and your hands touching the other two stems. While you are in this position, you close your eyes and imagine what you wish for. Make your intention clear; visualize it; and imagine that you send it up to the sky.

The birch tree will help you as its stems are channels between you and the sky. The birch tree makes your wish stronger and helps your wish to materialize faster.

This ritual... It immediately opens the doors to my soul and takes me simultaneously to multiple synchronicities from the past, to how the birch tree has been ever present at various turning points of my life.

FEBRUARY 2014,
Amsterdam (NL)

My son, my precious gift from the skies... Once upon a time, when I was a little girl, I always dreamt of having a son, a son who would be my best friend.

Years later, I wished to become a mother after healing my traumas. 'Be careful what you wish for', they say. For it took some healing time to make this wish come true. Little did I know back then, that it is a lifelong journey to heal your wounds...

Deep down inside, I still feel to this day that my son's soul joined us first in 2013. He came shortly and left me with the biggest healing clue: with the date I miscarried him.[16] May 2013, the Mother's Day I lost him was actually when I became a mother for the first time. It was also my moment of epiphany, a turning point in my healing journey.

---

[16] You may (re)read the story of this miscarriage on pp. 38-39.

The longer the healing journey takes, the more I start to ask myself whether this fertility journey has a purpose of its own in my soul's destiny. This embodied knowledge I have gained on these themes should not go to a waste. The feeling that I need to share what I have learned on the way grows. But how? Could this be leading me to my path as a healer?

With all these questions lurking in my mind, I receive a Tarot reading from my best friend Carolina on my birthday in February 2014. The reading points to a new path: to become a 'Mother of Mothers'.

A mother of mothers... That is what a doula[17] is, I swiftly conclude. After a quick online search, I find out that there is doula training in Amsterdam starting next week. Wow, that is fast! So fast that I do not feel quite ready yet for this big new step. I need some more time to get used to this idea of walking on this new path.

JULY 2014,
Rotterdam (NL)

I am ready now! I finally register for a Counseling & Coaching training to support mothers in their journeys to become pregnant *and* the doula training to support mothers around birth. This is how I will share my gift with the world! This is the path to the healer!

The day after: I am holding a positive pregnancy test in my hands. A day to remember,

---

17 A non-medical support person who assists women physically, practically, mentally, and psychologically during pregnancy, childbirth, and postpartum period.

forever. The day I received my biggest wish from the sky.

Years of trying, crying, healing... And finally seeing the two lines on the pregnancy test, for the third time. Yet this time I know; this time I trust that I will birth and hold this baby in my arms.

And with this synchronicity, I feel as if our son is now confident that I have started walking on my path, my path to become a healer.

With this precious confirmation from the skies in my belly, I start to walk on my path, to fulfill my destiny.

DECEMBER 2014,
Dordrecht (NL)

We have finally chosen our son's name, whilst welcoming the new year, the year we will meet him. We write his initial B in the sky, with fireworks.

BERKE – the name that has been calling me for months. A truly Turkish name, originating in Central Asia, the name of the grandson of Genghis Khan, Berke Khan, a name that stands for 'power and strength'.

A name that also exists in Dutch, derived from *berkenboom*, the birch tree in Dutch. And bonus dance for the fact that the name also exists in Frisian (the local language of the region my husband comes from) and means 'shining'.

The birch tree, a Nordic tree that thrives in colder climates and symbolizes new energy and new beginnings.

My son's name, to remind me forever of the gift he is of my healing and of my path as a healer.

Solar Eclipse, MARCH 2015,
Rotterdam (NL)

I am 38 weeks pregnant, and we are not expecting the birth to begin yet, but my son chooses his special day to "come through the portal" – as he will call it himself as 7-year-old when we talk about his day of birth.

This is not just an ordinary day. Today there is a total solar eclipse on the day of the equinox – a rare co-occurrence. A powerful day to mark a new beginning and to welcome the birth of the spring. The very last day of the astrological sign Pisces, too. My little wise boy, so longed for and so welcome.

What a day to give birth! As I cope with my contractions, I suddenly rise up without a word and move to the dining room. I reach out for the bracelet that my circle of women have made for me during my blessingway ceremony.[18] I hold on to my bracelet and lean on the female power and intentions embodied in every bead. It is at that very moment that the sky turns dark. The solar eclipse reaches its highest point, and my contractions start getting stronger.

OCTOBER 2015,
Rotterdam (NL)

My son can already sit on his own and has his first teeth. And I am ready to gradually come out of my postpartum cocoon.

---

[18] A ceremony to honor pregnant women before they become mothers based on the Navajo Indian traditions of North America.

I have just attended my first birth as a doula. Pure magic: the birthing space, the birthing energy, all the love, all the oxytocin. I know right away: I will doula as long as my body will allow me to!

After supporting this first birth, I decide to take concrete steps to set up my business. I need a name for my company. My heart goes for 'birch', as a salute to my son and as a word that rhymes with birth. I register birch.nl, or so I think until the webhosting company sends me a warning saying that this domain name is already registered by a company with the same name. Error and change of plans!

I close my eyes for inspiration for a new name: 'Birth Wish' comes through. I immediately fall in love with it and start to play with the name. 'Your Birth, Your Wish' my motto. Make your wishes come true. Yes! Let's go birthwish.nl!

APRIL 2020,
Rotterdam (NL)

My friend Carolina is doing a small research on neo-shamanism. She shares the results of this research with me for feedback, together with some resources and books. The researcher in me dives right into the world of shamanism with full curiosity.

One of the first things I stumble upon is that the birch tree is considered to be tree of shamans in Siberia. It is the tree they use to build their drums with and the tree on which they are "buried" when they die.

Goosebumps. My son, my shamanic path. The birch tree opens a new door again, the door to the shamanic chapter of my life.

In all shamanic legends there is a tree – a larch, spruce, or birch tree. And the whole life of the shaman, from birth to death, is connected with this tree.

According to the Yakut legend, the supreme deity Aya Toyon planted three trees. Sitting at their base, he prepared all the attributes for the first shaman, and then taught him how to act for the benefit of the people in the fight against evil spirits. Yakutians believed that the souls of future shamans were brought up on this sacred tree in the form of little birds.

When a person grows up to become a shaman, the rim of his drum is made from a piece of wood, while the bird spirits fly to the shamanic pillar. Shamans do not get their drum immediately. Spirits allow them to use the drum while they are in shamanic trance. A spirit tells them about the structure of their drum and shows them the tree from which a drum should be made. Typically, this is a birch tree, and only a piece of wood is taken from it, so that the tree does not die.

The shaman's drum is covered with leather; it is painted, and metal pendants are attached to it. When the drum is ready, then the ritual of instrument reviving is performed. An animal, the skin of which is wrapped around a drum, becomes the patron spirit of the drum, and the shaman can ride it in the world of spirits. The drum contains the external soul of a shaman in the guise of an animal and is the personification of shamanic strength and life.

JULY 2016,
Zhivo (RUS)

Germaine travels to Siberia for the second time. Even though she has already followed Ahamkara's shamanic healer training twice (once live and once online), she still does not have a drum of her own. In Zhivo, the other students buy drums, but she insists that she does not want one. Ahamkara has to laugh about Germaine's resistance.

Then one night, as Germaine is lying in bed, she has a vision about a beautiful tree. It comes closer and closer. Germaine realizes this is the shamanic tree. Then she also sees a very beautiful drum hanging there on one of the tree's branches. After this dream, she knows that she now has to have a drum of her own.

When Germaine tells about her dream to Ahamkara, he says: "It is time. The drum is calling you."

She takes one of Ahamkara's drums to which she feels drawn to. She holds it. She becomes one with it. They are finally united: Germaine and her drum.

Not everyone needs to travel to Siberia to meet their drum. Those with a shamanic calling mostly meet theirs during their shamanic training.

SHAMANIC TRAINING

Shamanic learning and growth lasts a lifetime, but the first stages of shamanic formation constitute the most important phase. A mentor must accompany the novice to introduce them to spiritual secrets, to guide them through the ways of building a new personality, to show them the ways to other worlds, and to warn them about the dangers that arise while performing a ritual.

A shaman receives recognition only after undergoing dual apprenticeship: given both by the spirits in the form of dreams, visions, and trance instructions, as well as by experienced shamans who transmit shamanic techniques and knowledge about the spirits. Such apprenticeship, which sometimes takes place publicly, is equivalent to an initiation ritual. However, this ritual can also take place without the involvement of other people, during sleep or in trance states.

The shamanic teachings of Altai shamanism have a verbal tradition. There are no written statements of its foundations, provisions, or declarations. Neither are there are any canonical rules, commandments, prohibitions, texts of prayers, etc. All teaching is given on an oral-visual basis and by using simple ritual props. There is no professional hierarchical specialization based on certain rituals and trials that shamans must undergo during their training on Altai shamanism.

Shamanic training in the Altai is not that easy and requires not only physical endurance, but also spiritual devotion. Initiation begins with a long period of preparation and purification. The disciples spend weeks in deep forests or on mountain tops, isolated from the world around them. They only eat herbs and roots, spend days and nights in meditation and prayer, preparing their spirit to meet the spiritual world.

After this initiation, the training on the basic techniques of shamanic practice starts: establishing contact with nature spirits, working with energies, and healing the body and spirit. The apprentice goes through trials and tests of their strength and of their faith in their ability to become a true shaman.

The rituals during this training can be frightening at times. The trainee receives visions, hears spirit voices, and experiences ecstasy and terror at the same time. They immerse themselves in the world of shadows and dreams, seek answers to questions about life and death, and prepare themselves to become an intermediary between the world of the living and the spirits.

2001-2002,
Gorno-Altaysk (RUS)

Ahamkara accepts the invitation of his teacher Shaman Arzhan to join his shamanic training in the Altai. This is when he leaves his comfortable life, family, and friends in the city behind to walk his shamanic path in a small village of the Altai.

From that moment on, the journey to drink and grow from his teacher's well of wisdom begins. The name of his shaman teacher literally means

well/source, and he embodies this name in his teaching philosophy. Ahamkara envisions his teacher like a waterfall flowing from a mountain top, pouring and sharing his wisdom with his students.

The first year of training in the Altai is all about learning and discipline. Bootcamp elements such as running and swimming in ice-cold water are regular parts of the shamanic training.

Fasting occupies an important place in the physical training, both as a method of detoxing and self-healing. They practice with up to seven days of fasting in a row. Fasting is not a regular practice, but the real difficulty lies in the fact that the fasting starts suddenly at the initiative of the teacher.

Ahamkara finds these "surprise fasting episodes" quite challenging. He does not know when the fasting will begin and when it will end. He has no control over it. This actually constitutes the core of the training of the shaman student in Siberia: Trust the teacher and surrender fully.

Shamanic training has one core purpose: to contribute to an individual's growth and development. Siberian shamanic training emphasizes building personal power and the ability to overcome obstacles in life. It is quite tough and somewhat comparable to joining a monastery. You have to follow your teacher. In this sense, it is also about training your ego by trusting your teacher's judgment and instructions.

There is always a level of distance between the teacher and the student which should be kept to ensure respect. The teacher and the student should neither be too close, nor become friends. Otherwise, students start to teach the teacher.

Trusting and respecting the teacher helps the student to learn faster. This does not mean, however, that the student remains a student forever. The role of the student is comparable to that of a child: The student takes and absorbs all the information that is provided by the teacher until they have grown up enough to use it on their own two feet.

2005-2006,
Valthe (NL)

Mura joins the shamanic healer training offered by Ahamkara in the Netherlands. This really feels like coming home for her. She has already read a lot of spiritual books, but this is different: It all feels right, and all things finally seem to fall into place.

She absorbs the training like a sponge. And what she enjoys the most is that Ahamkara acts so 'ordinary': He just sits down with the group and starts telling his story, whereas with the other shamans she had encountered, she had always felt as if they were sitting in their throne and telling "the kids" to listen to them. Ahamkara just simply tells his story, and this actually makes him special.

2007,
Valthe (NL)

After Mura completes her shamanic year training, she signs up for the shamanic death ceremonies led by him since she is still craving for more shamanism.

Around the same time, Ahamkara parts his ways with the assistant he had been working with for his events and teaching in the Netherlands. The owner of the then spiritual center Mirre, where Ahamkara's trainings are held, asks Mura whether she would like to become the new assistant.

For Mura, it is a huge step to ask Ahamkara if he would like her to become his assistant. She finally summons her courage to ask him. She waits anxiously for his response. The reply is short and clear: "Yes."

From that moment on, Mura assists Ahamkara during his trainings and events in the Netherlands for nine years. These years of assisting him were never boring, as she kept on learning something new every time.

It is sometimes challenging to be Ahamkara's assistant. He always tunes in with the energy of the group, so the plans can suddenly change. This teaches Mura to become flexible and to be always prepared to light a fire, for example. She always had candles, newspapers, matches, etc. with her for a fire ceremony or to warm up the drum for a ritual.

During her years as an assistant, Mura felt like a student, but this was rather her own feeling than how Ahamkara made her feel. He actually asked her to lead the ceremonies now and then, so that she could practice with the group. During the ceremonies led by her, he just participated as a member of the group and did not interfere with the process. These experiences allowed her to slowly grow into her role as a teacher as she gradually started to offer her own shamanic ceremonies, courses, and year training.

2008,
Assen (NL)

Ahamkara stays at Mura's house during his teaching days in the north of the Netherlands. By now, Mura has already been assisting him for a year, but she is still longing to learn more and go deeper in her shamanic path.

When Mura brings Ahamkara to the train station in Assen after his stay at their place, she needs to gather all her courage again, this time to ask him to become his personal student.

She first gives Ahamkara a hug on the platform as he steps into the train. Before he moves on to take his seat in the train, Mura manages to find her words with a racing heart: "I have one last question: May I become your personal student?"

"All right!" Ahamkara says, "and your first lesson is: Face your fears!" And the train doors close before Mura finds the time to reply. Perfect divine timing!

Mura is left behind thinking: 'Shit! This is not what I wanted to hear!' But she knows deep down that she has to take up this task, even though she does not like her "homework" at all.

Fear has been a dominant theme in her life for years, and she knows that she now has to face it. Ahamkara actually never gives her a lesson or a homework on facing her fears. He just observes what she does, what she says, and what she asks.

Time and again, he tunes into what she is willing to do and what she needs. This means in practice that Mura has to take the initiative herself, and this is scary in and of itself! He really challenges her in that sense.

Mura sometimes calls Ahamkara for advice on various problems in her life, and sometimes all he says is: "Fear constrains."

During these years as his personal student, it was never a lesson or teaching as she would have expected, but she learns a lot, just by observing what is happening and by having to take all the steps herself.

APRIL 2020,
Rotterdam (NL)

I had wished for a spiritual retreat in 2020 on the falling stars of the summer of 2019, and the opportunity represents itself exactly when I feel ready to take the next step on my shamanic path.

I buy my plane tickets. I make all the arrangements, book a babysitter for the kids. I am ready to fly to Türkiye for a forest retreat in my father's birth town Bolu. My roots are calling me.

Then: worldwide lockdown happens; all flights are cancelled, and everyone is thrown into a surreal, virtual world, locked into their screens and houses.

In the meantime, nature is in the greatest contrast with the empty, dead streets. The sun is constantly shining; the trees have their greenest leaves popping out; the fields are full with wild flowers.

I also go with the flow of the new phenomenon of online webinars and circles. It is time to sit still and do some self-care and healing all over the world it seems.

I stumble upon the call of a fellow space holder in Türkiye, Filiz who bravely calls out for what we most need to do collectively: grieve. I would never imagine an online grieving circle could be so powerful. I cry for all the shared grief and start reading Francis Weller's masterpiece on grief, *The Wild Edge of Sorrow*.[19]

Grief... A topic I carry in my cells, a topic I have been introduced to way too early as an 8-year-old, a topic that keeps on knocking on my door time and again.

I ride the layers of grief, my grief, the grief of my ancestors, the grief of the world. And then I hear my calling again, my calling to serve and heal the world. I feel the time has come to go to the next level in following my soul's path – the path I did not dare to walk right away when I put my diplomas and academic career aside to follow my heart.

Back then I had said to my friend Carolina: "I wish I could become a shamanic healer when I grow up." It felt like this was the highest point one

---

[19] Francis Weller (2015) *The Wild Edge of Sorrow: Rituals of Renewal and the Sacred Work of Grief*. North Atlantic Books.

could reach in terms of becoming a healer, and I was not feeling I was quite there yet.

Carolina now gives me the memoir of the British shaman Ya'acov Darling Khan[20] for inspiration. I start reading the book and feel a bit overwhelmed about what it takes to walk the shamanic path. How on earth can I possibly walk this path now as a mother of two small kids?

I keep on searching further. I stumble upon past shamanic gatherings with shamans from all around the world organized in the Netherlands. That must have been awesome. And here we are in the middle of lockdowns. For the time being, there will be no shamans travelling to the Netherlands and no shamanic teaching festivals being organized, I realize. *Which shamanism and shaman should I turn to now?*

My initial research also allows me to realize how shamanistic rituals and traditions have been integrated into the Turkish culture. I suddenly get a flashback of the first history lesson at primary school, still deeply engrained in my memory, of the Central Asian origins of history.

I feel the call to stay close to my roots, to my Turkish and Central Asian roots. I choose for Siberian shamanism, and I want to learn it live. I want to experience shamanism physically first. This path leads me to the Institute of Siberian Shamanism in the Netherlands.

---

[20] Ya'acov Darling Khan (2017) *Jaguar in the Body, Butterfly in the Heart: The Real-Life Initiation of an Everyday Shaman.* Hay House.

SEPTEMBER 2021,
Rotterdam (NL)

I run into the call of year training of the Institute of Siberian Shamanism on my timeline in Facebook, announcing that they will offer their year training courses on Fridays this year. Friday is my husband's day off work, so I decide to stop postponing my dream and to start my shamanic training, despite the fact that this is financially not an ideal time for this investment.

I contact the teacher, and we book an online meeting. I am moved by this first meeting with Petra (Altaiskaya Byelka), especially by the messages from Spirit she shares with me during this call:

> Spirit is very much present on your path. You have qualities which assist you in your path. You are sensitive. Spirituality is a gift you were born with. Your channels were already open when you were born, and you did not have to dust everything off or to open your channels. They were open, and they remained open. There are a few more things that can open up more, but what you have is a great advantage for you.

Wow! I get goosebumps all over my body when I hear this. I feel grateful to be born with this gift, and not to have damaged it along the way.

> When I ask Spirit how this shamanic training can contribute to your personal growth, Spirit says it will strengthen your self-confidence and enable you to connect your Turkish roots with who you are as a person. Your roots will become a part of your whole being, instead of being something separate from you.

> Spirit says that through the training, you will understand some of the things you do automatically more thoroughly. This will give you more self-confidence, and you will be able to add this knowledge to your current repertoire.
>
> Spirit says that you can focus very well on every person you connect with and open your heart to them. You can build on this skill, deepen it, and expand it by learning to work with spirit helpers, using more energy work, for yourself, for your kids, and the women you work with. Spirit adds that you will be very comfortable working with the rituals you learn throughout the training.

With this fantastic introduction to the world of spirits, I feel honored, ready, and excited to start my first shamanic training. This message is such an important confirmation that this is my path, and that entering the world of shamanism will allow me to go back to my roots and origins. It tells me that I am not starting from scratch. I am just coming back home, for good.

SEPTEMBER 2021,
Etten-Leur (NL)

The first day of the shamanic training. We go into our first trance to meet our power animal. Can this be this easy or am I only "dreaming"?

Noticing my doubt, the teacher comes to me and tells me: "Trust what you see."

If this is true, travelling to the dream world is really like second nature to me. I close my eyes, and I am in trance. Just like that. I first need to let this natural gift sink in.

OCTOBER 2021,
Etten-Leur (NL)

During the introduction call, our teacher has also shares which spirit animal has appeared to her as my power animal. I am pretty surprised that I receive the lizard. This is not particularly an animal I have ever felt connected with. As I read about lizards and connect with their energy though, I start to feel their special energy and enjoy working with this spirit.

Next lesson, our teacher tells us that it is handy to have a part of your spirit animal to use as extra support during healings. And at that very moment, I get a flashback to the summer holidays in my parents' summerhouse outside Istanbul, where I had found a decapitated lizard on the terrace near the garden. It attracted my attention, but I had not picked it up.

Had the lizard already presented itself to me as a spirit guide? And had I just left it lying there?! I now regretted my choice, but it was too late. Yet, the memory of the lizard helps me to become even more attached to this special spirit animal.

JANUARY 2022,
Rotterdam (NL)

My shamanic drum has arrived. When I visualized my drum in the dream world, it came with a Turkic sky blue spiral on it. A Turkish shamanic practitioner made it from mountain goat skin and beech tree and dried it in the Turkish sun.

Piece of home that I bring to the Netherlands safely in its cover. With my drum in my hands, I search for a YouTube instruction film on how to connect with the spirit of the drum and how to greet and bless it before starting to use it for the first time.

The information I am looking for, I find on the YouTube page I discover of the Siberian Shaman Ahamkara. Wow, what a loving positive energy!

I browse further and see that Ahamkara has an online shamanic healer training, and it immediately goes on my wish list. In the meantime, I start watching the online teachings he generously shares.

And I cannot help but notice a sign: Ahamkara often wears a blue shirt with a spiral on it.

APRIL 2022,
Rotterdam (NL)

Ahamkara is in the Netherlands. I look up all the organized events and locations. I am really interested in his one-day organ massage course. Or should I go to him for a healing? In any case, I feel that I have to meet him personally.

In the end, we agree on an online meeting during his stay in Drenthe. I ask him for guidance on my shamanic path. He leaves the choice to me, as to how I should pursue my shamanic path and advises me to already practice what I have been learning by offering healings.

And he adds: "You can always contact me for questions or advice."

I know right away after this meeting that he is the shamanic teacher I am seeking. I somehow take for granted that I will meet him for real, not realizing yet that it might take years.

For starters, I join Ahamkara's five-day online training *Shamanism for Beginners*. The five rituals during this training speak deeply to my dream body. I definitely want to learn more from him, and I know it is just a matter of when, not if.

MARCH 2024,
Luxwoude (NL)

After completing Ahamkara's online organ massage course in 2023, I focus on raising my entrepreneurship skills. I take some marketing courses in the hope of making a fresh start in Friesland. I have to literally build up my network from scratch and to build up my website's algorithm anew. Yet after six months of applying all the tips and tricks, I still do not see tangible results.

What do I do now? Why is nothing working out? I feel defeated. Then I suddenly recall a story Ahamkara told about his own path during one of his lectures: The business initiatives that were not related to his shamanic path did not turn out well, whereas all his initiatives linked to his shamanic destiny progressed easily.

What if this is a sign that it is now time to take the next step on my shamanic path and to finally go for Ahamkara's year training? I know that his new year training group has just started at the end of February. I have missed a few lessons already, but there is a bigger obstacle on my way: I still have not managed to earn enough money to finance the training.

Moment of truth: I need to ask Ahamkara for assistance. But how?

I call my friend Marite. She suggests that I offer him a service in return for the training and adds: "Look at your CV! What are you good at? What would you like to do for him?"

And right there on the spot, I get a wild idea: What if I help Ahamkara write a book on shamanism and his shamanic path?

After I hang up the phone, I send a mail to him explaining my situation and presenting my idea of receiving the online training in return for assisting him in his work, for his trainings, his administration, or: for writing a book on his life and shamanism. I click the send button and go out for a walk in the forest nearby our house.

Magic follows swiftly. First, I encounter a herd of five deer on the field near the forest. It is not the first time I meet deer here, but it is the first time I see five of them together. I return home mesmerized and search the meaning of seeing five deer and find:

> When we see five deer, it may be a sign that we are being guided towards our life's purpose, passion, or spiritual path. It is a reminder to trust in the universe's plan and have faith that everything is working in our favor.

The five deer signal the good news that is about to arrive. Shortly after Ahamkara replies: "Book is an interesting idea. Let's meet and talk."

We exchange some messages, and the book idea already starts to evolve. Ahamkara says "Yes" and thinks it is also a great plan that I join the

training which will also help me in writing the book.

This is more than I could ever wish and dream for! It feels like all my life paths come together; as if I can finally reap the fruits of all these years of studying, learning, writing, and healing. It is now time to shine!

As soon as I begin the training, I am amazed by the depth of Ahamkara's training. With every lesson, I learn to feel the spirits and to live with the spirits. Day by day, shamanistic living and rituals become a part of my life.

And on top of all this wisdom, I now have regular contact with Ahamkara on the book. I feel truly blessed.

FULFILLING YOUR DESTINY & SHARING SHAMANIC WISDOM

When you take the shamanic path, the intention is to grow and to learn to take responsibility yourself. If the teacher keeps you dependent on them, you remain a student forever and travel from training to training as a mere "spiritual tourist".

At some point, the student needs to come out of this role, find the answers themselves, and take responsibility. The student should not be attached to the energy of the teacher. The aim of shamanic training is to teach the students to become teachers themselves.

Ahamkara's initial challenge as a healer is self-doubt. This feeling had been with him all his life. He strongly doubted whether he would be able to help people with his healings and whether he would be able to answer their questions.

In the beginning, he is moreover very worried about how people will perceive him as a shaman. Later on he becomes concerned about how he would conduct rituals in public. It takes several years to get rid of all his uncertainty. It was really difficult and scary, but he continues to practice and gradually frees himself from these fears.

After Ahamkara completes his studies with his teacher in the Altai, he starts treating people and helping them solve various problems. Once he starts practicing as a healer, he almost immediately realizes that it is not enough to give people treatments and healings. He needs to share his knowledge with them about how health problems arise and how they can prevent them from arising in the first place.

His urge to teach people leads him to start giving seminars. First, these are short, one to two day teachings, focusing only on a few topics. These seminars eventually grow into a whole year training.

At the age of 27, Ahamkara travels to Europe for the first time and organizes his first training seminar there. It is in Paris, and he does not speak French. He finds a translator, makes an announcement, and the first group gathers. He is very worried, but everything goes well, and the participants are happy.

That is how he starts giving seminars in Europe, and his first students begin to ask whether they can receive a deeper and longer training on Altai shamanism. That is how he starts contemplating about a large annual shamanism training program.

At that time, online education is not that popular yet. He meets with students live, seven times a year, and each meeting lasts two days. During these days, he shares his knowledge and answers questions, and between the meetings, the students do a lot of homework.

He teaches students in this manner for about fifteen years while he keeps on improving and refining his teaching methods. Hundreds of students follow his shamanic training program. Most students come to initially solve their own problems, and after the training they also start to help others.

During these seminars in Europe, many people ask for the annual program, but they often do not have the opportunity to come to Ahamkara's teachings. By then, online education is already beginning to develop, and he starts thinking about how he could conduct his training online.

It is a very difficult task for him to develop online teaching as this is a completely different way of training. It has its pros and cons. In 2019, Ahamkara launches the first volume of his online training program and invites everyone who has ever expressed the wish to study with him, but have not been able to join his trainings.

The first online group of students is very friendly. They communicate a lot amongst themselves during the training and continue to stay in contact after the completion of the year program. Many students have become friends and still meet each other.

The results of the first volume of the online training are very inspiring. Many students give good feedback and point out that their lives have changed a lot throughout that year of shamanic training.

When the global pandemic begins, it seems that the circumstances in the world are insurmountable. Everyone abandons their plans to travel and to hold mass events. At first, Ahamkara also succumbs to this global tension and gloom. Soon he realizes that he has to move towards his goals and trust his power, spirits, and the world.

He decides to travel, arrives at the border and does not know if they will let him go through. They do not let him cross the border that day. Two days later, he tries to cross the border again, and this time they let him go through. He refuses to be stopped by circumstances and keeps on walking on his shamanic path.

Ahamkara feels that shamanism is his destiny, that he has had to follow this path. Looking back now, he understands that the spirits have led him to this point all his life. When he did something other than shamanism, he had no joy and happiness, and often his undertakings were destroyed by Spirit. To the contrary, everything he has undertaken that was related to shamanism tended to go very well and with ease.

He feels a lot of fulfillment when he sees people solving their problems, and their lives change for the better. Interestingly, the students who ever came to him with the biggest problems in their lives and managed to solve these problems, became strong healers themselves. Their own negative experiences, together with their experience of treatment and healing with the help of shamanism, helped them to understand their own clients with similar problems better.

Germaine's biggest hurdle on her shamanic path is accepting her gifts as a healer and learning to work with her gifts, instead of being overwhelmed by them. Learning from and working intensively with Ahamkara helped her first to heal herself and afterwards to follow her path as a healer.

Before she ended up at the psychiatry ward, she did not even want to touch anything anymore because she was hearing messages from spirits all the time – from flowers, from food, from stones.

Her tongue was also constantly in trance. It was giving messages on and on, all day long. She had to embrace her tongue as one of her gifts as a healer. Ahamkara guided her in using her tongue, and she came to accept it as her talent. Her tongue is virtually connected to the universe.

Germaine hears a lot of spirits around her who talk to her. Ahamkara first teaches her how to bring the spirits of deceased people to the light. She also learns how to bring her trance under control. Ahamkara is the first person who really helps her with all these issues. She trusts him right away because she feels that he is pure.

Ahamkara recognizes her gift immediately and treated her as a shaman and not like she is mentally ill. He knows that many people in psychiatric hospitals are gifted, but that doctors do not know how to deal with them, as nobody has taught them how. Often the medical system does not know anything about shamanism. Unknowingly, by giving psychiatric pills, they suppress people's shamanic gifts and connection to the spiritual world.

For shamans like Germaine, the separation between the dream world and material world is minimal. Germaine's connection with the dream world is so strong that the border between the two worlds is very thin for her. When you have such a gift, it is tricky if you perceive the dream world as the material world. When you do not have the power to control such a gift, your gift can also destroy you.

The next task is to teach Germaine to trust in what the spirit world wants from her. Once she accepts her shamanic path, she starts hearing place names in the middle of the night, like Jaffa (Israel) and Petra (Jordan). She has visions of her previous lives there. In one of her visions of Petra, she is guided by a woman in black clothes, who makes a fire and initiates her into her new path as a healer.

She also has visions of Findhorn (Scotland). She realizes she has lived there as a druid/witch in a previous life. Through connecting with her past life in Findhorn, all the magic and wisdom of this place comes through. She makes contact with the elves, gnomes, and nymphs.

Besides the empowering positive past life memories, Germaine also experiences being held back by traumas originating from past lives. She once says to Ahamkara: "I cannot do this work because I will be brought to court." This is actually just a vision from a previous life, but she is so scared that she feels the need to receive an official training to practice safely as a healer.

To begin with she wants to learn organ massage, as she realizes that the organs talk to her when she does healings. She follows a three-year training in Rotterdam and receives her diploma for organ massage. She also completes the shamanic healer year trainings with Ahamkara. This is all to receive the reassurance she needs, so that she can embrace her power and share her talents and gifts as a healer.

When they finally move out of the café as a family to live in a house with a garden, she also has a stall with donkeys, next to which she sets up her healing practice, Stalletje de Merk. As she starts offering shamanic healings combined with organ massage, her practice grows with the word of mouth.

As Germaine is also a medium, she connects her clients with their deceased loved ones. There is one case she will never forget: the parents of a deceased little girl called Marley. After Marley dies, her parents divorce and lose their direction in life. Her father has a burnout; he is not able to work and loses his willingness to live. Deep down inside, he is feeling guilty that he has not been there enough for Marley. Marley had cancer. While she was staying at the pediatric hospital, she had been really strong, but she unfortunately lost her life.

After her death, it was first Marley's father who came to Germaine for help. Her mother followed suit. Marley had very strong messages for her parents, about her illness, but also about their relationship. The messages Germaine received from the little Marley were so powerful that they helped the parents to find their strength again to move forward in life and to reawaken their life energy.

Being able to help people through her gift makes Germaine happy. For her, this is above all a way to spread the love from the spirits which she sees, hears, and feels all around her.

I am still on my way, walking my shamanic path. I am choosing more and more for my spiritual mission. I am learning to walk the walk and talk the talk.

It is sometimes easier said than done. Often, it is also a matter of overcoming my own barriers, my own shadows, after years of being on the healing path: There is always more to heal.

By now, I feel I have the necessary tools to heal others, yet there is still something holding me back from standing up as a healer. Maybe that is not even necessary, for we sometimes heal with a simple word, with a daily conversation, with a loving act.

Do I always need a drum or a ritual to heal? Or is it more about being fully present, feeling, seeing, and holding space?

What I do know by now is that rituals give comfort and make it easier to connect both to our inner wisdom and to memories of ancestral wisdom. We definitely need more rituals. We definitely need more stories. We need to bring them back to our daily life. And this has been the biggest gift of Ahamkara's year training for me.

Through Ahamkara's teachings, I have learned to weave shamanism into my whole life, into my way of living, looking, seeing in the world.

Shamanism is a powerful way of living. It is grounded and holistic, and it empowers individuals to help themselves. After all, this has been my mission all along: to help people discover the power within themselves.

My core mission as a healer is clear. Yet, I sometimes still feel I lack the tools to share my gifts with more ease. The flow that I feel just as I write these words... I wish this would spread to all areas of my life.

Maybe writing is my healing gift after all. Maybe it is just a matter of time. Maybe it is all about trusting that everything falls into its place when the time is ripe. And also becoming aware of everything being perfect as they are, becoming aware that every step is a stepping stone to our next step on our shamanic path. One next step that is surely on my wish list is travelling to Siberia.

THE SPIRIT of SIBERIA

Going to the origins, to the homeland of shamanism to Siberia to live and breathe this vast land, starting from the Ural Mountains in the west and stretching through thousands of kilometers up to the Pacific Ocean in the east. Siberia, the vast territory embodying unimaginable body of natural beauty and wonders. The Altai, the cradle of civilizations, Siberia's heart of sacred power and vital energy.

Since ancient times, the culture, traditions, and worldview of the Altai people have been inextricably connected with nature and living in harmony with it. It is a place where you feel and love nature with all your heart and soul, and nature embraces and supports you. When you are in the Altai, you hear nature's breath and nature's responses inside yourself. It is a temple of wisdom, where every flower and river multiplies the energy of your thoughts.

The Legend of Altai

In ancient times, there lived the rich and powerful Khan Altai. The best herds and tracts belonged to this Khan; the most noble and strongest warriors served him. But Altai considered his beautiful daughter Katun to be his greatest wealth. Katun was proud and independent. Her young beauty captivated many heroes, but Katun did not give any of them her affectionate gaze and did not even smile once to anyone.

Katun loved to go to the steppe on her fast horse. One day, while traveling across the steppe, she met a young man named Biy. So beautiful and statuesque was the young man, so agile was he in the saddle, that the proud Katun fell in love with him. Biy also took a liking to the steppe beauty. From that moment on, they often rode together across the steppe and breathed in the fragrant smells of the herbs and flowers.

Biy was not rich. And Altai did not like the young man, so he felt it was time to marry off his beloved daughter. He gathered the richest and strongest warriors from all over the world.

Katun told her father, however, that he had forgotten to invite a *batyr* (brave warrior) called Biy.

Altai became very angry when he heard this name and announced to everyone that at dawn, when the sun would gild the earth and the sky from the east, he himself would call the name of the chosen one for his daughter.

Katun's heart could not put up with this decision of the Khan. At night, when Altai fell asleep and when all the warriors and the guards fell asleep, she secretly saddled her horse and ran away to Biy.

In the morning, having discovered his daughter's disappearance, the Khan raised his warriors and told them: "Whoever is the first of you to catch up with Katun and return her to her father's yurt will become her husband!"

The warriors rushed after the Khan's daughter. But the Khan realized that they could not catch up with her. Then he cursed everything in the world! This curse began to turn everything around him into stone: The Khan's yurt was petrified, and on the place where it once stood, Mount Belukha was formed. The ranks of the galloping warriors were also petrified, turning into the Altai Mountains.

Only Biy and Katun were not touched by the Khan's curse because they loved each other and strived to unite. Biy and Katun continued their path together. And on the path where they traveled, fresh rivers were formed: the bright and wide Biy and the playful, unbridled Katun. To this day, the two rivers meet and kiss each other at the river Ob.

The Call of Mount Belukha

Belukha Mountain, the highest point of the Altai Mountains, is the main place of power for Altai shamans. Since ancient times, it is considered as a sacred place in Asia. According to the legend, it is the northern *Shambala* – a mythical kingdom symbolizing a place of peace and happiness. Ancient legends claim that the "**Navel of the Earth**" lies on this mountain which is energetically connected with the cosmos, giving people power, courage, and health and helping them discover new knowledge.

When you are in the Altai, you feel and breathe in the wisdom and power of the Earth. You go to the Altai to unite with nature, to talk to it, and to learn from it. In the Altai, you are surrounded by spirits all around. No wonder so much wisdom has been born here, and no wonder why it has attracted so many soul seekers.

Travelling to the Altai is a pilgrim's journey, a journey to meet the spirit of Siberia: the wise old man holding the wisdom of the world. It is a journey to meet yourself on the bright and dark sides.

SUMMER 2013,
Altai (RUS)

Mura has been dreaming of travelling to the Altai for years. When they buy the church to transform it into their spiritual center, they end up investing all their savings in the construction work. Mura's Altai dream seems further away than ever, until one day in the winter of 2012 when Mura's mother comes to bring her a surprise and says:

> You always wanted to go to Russia, right? I would have also liked to go there, but I cannot anymore. I am too sick to travel. So what would you say if I give you some money from your grandfather's inheritance? I had put it aside for this journey anyways, so I would like to pay this journey for you. How much does it cost?

Mura accepts her mother's exciting offer right away. This feels like a gift from the heavens and opens the door to what will become her karmic journey to the sacred lands of the Altai.

When Ahamkara hears the news, he asks her to also support him during this journey. Mura's task is to assist him spiritually but also to help with cooking, taking care of any wounds, and to help with the social dynamics of the group.

When the journey in Siberia begins, Mura is fulfilling her role as an assistant and focusing on serving the group. She still has the feeling that Ahamkara is the teacher, and she is the student. This is again not because of how Ahamkara treats her or makes her feel, but rather because of her own inner feeling of insecurity and fear of making mistakes.

On the third day they are travelling to the Altai with an old bus, it begins to rain with thunderstorms. As Mura is searching for a tent where she will take shelter, she hears Ahamkara calling her name. Her place is in the bus with him, the bus driver, and Ahamkara's Russian-Dutch friend Jasja, who is also there to support the group with translating, cooking, and carrying the supplies where needed.

When she hops on the bus and sits next to Ahamkara, she suddenly feels the comradeship. They sit there eating nuts and honey and making jokes. This is the moment when she finally feels united and equal with the team.

She realizes that this is also one of the lessons she has to learn: to let go of the idea of rank and status, the idea she has internalized deeply in her upbringing: 'The doctor and the pastor are the important people. They know it while you are just an ordinary little person.'

Looking back, she sees that the thunderstorm carried the energy of transformation and blessing from Tengri for her. From that moment on, she could be more herself during this journey, despite the fact that she was still assisting Ahamkara.

When the journey takes the group to where the rivers Katun and Biy meet at the Ob, they are invited to build a wish tower from stones: The bigger your wish, the higher your tower should be. Next to her individual wish tower, Mura also builds a tower with Ahamkara where their common ideas and wishes symbolically come together.

One of Mura's intentions with her journey to the Altai is to heal their family's health issues with weak knees and lung diseases. While hiking through the Altai mountains, she keeps on asking for help from Spirit every time her knees hurt so much that she experiences trouble keeping up with the group.

The journey through the Altai takes them from one sacred place to another, from sacred springs to trees. Every place is impressive. Finally, they reach the village of Tungur, which means drum in the Altai language. This is where you cross the bridge and arrive at sacred territory. Before the bridge, it is still inhabited, but thereafter the magic grows even bigger.

In the Netherlands, if you want to pass over to the magical world of spirits, you need to open a thick curtain with great force to the side to be able to set a foot through. There, in the Altai, the curtain is thin, more like a net curtain. Sometimes the net curtain is so old that it pulverizes the moment you want to set a foot through.

Sometimes, the magic even comes to you whether you ask for it or not. It is important to remain conscious and to stay in balance in case Spirit wants to test how strong you are standing in your shoes.

While you are climbing the mountain, it gets cold and hard. And Mura has to gather her strength, not only for herself, but also to keep the group together and going. At one point, she is leading the horseback riding group while Ahamkara is leading the hiking group. By then, they have reached the part of the journey where there is no cellphone connection. The group is exhausted and cold and wants to get back to the basecamp, but they need to continue their journey.

As Mura cannot reach Ahamkara, she has to rely on her own strength and guidance to keep the group moving.

It is a harsh journey after all. It is a real pilgrimage. You do not go on this journey just for fun. Mura is relieved when the whole group manages to reach the first glacier of Belukha to camp there.

The next morning, she wakes up early to perform a ritual to thank her ancestors and her mother. This is one of the reasons why she came here, and if it were not for their support, she would not be in Siberia.

She asks for a sign from the spirits. While she is walking, she sees a heart-shaped stone in the water. She picks up the stone and puts it in her pocket. Then she gathers more stones to draw a big heart. In the middle of the heart, she writes the family name of her mother. While doing so, she realizes she has made a spelling error which she corrects afterwards. She finds out later on, that precisely at the same moment, her mother has also made a spelling mistake at the notary while signing the documents for her testament!

At the glacier, they meet other people who are also on a pilgrimage journey. The group receives a warm welcome from them, and when Mura wants to warm the drum for a ritual, they are happy to help her out. She feels so supported and held by these people who were total strangers. Another member of this group also gives Mura and the whole group pieces of petrified snow as a gift, as a souvenir from the Altai. Thinking back to all these beautiful moments still brings tears to Mura's eyes.

On the way back, the group goes to the *banya* where Mura receives the unforgettable birch branch massage for karmic healing from Ahamkara.[21] At the end of this trip to the Altai, Mura also receives her shamanic initiation from Ahamkara.

On the last evening of the trip, before they drive out of the Altai, Ahamkara says: “It is now the time Mura. Pack your sleeping bag, warm clothes, and a plastic sheet to cover the ground.” They start walking for what it feels like ages. Finally, they reach a place where Ahamkara says: “Yes, this is a good place.”

Here there is water and four trees to guard her. It is here that she receives her initiation during which she promises to serve the community, humanity, nature, harmony and balance, herself, her environment, the world, the universe, and the spirits.

Before Ahamkara leaves Mura to spend the night on her own in nature, he reminds her that she can always come back to the group if she is scared. That would only mean that she is not up for this quest yet. If that is the case, she may always try again later.

Mura knows by now that fear is always related to attachments. She enters the night on her own and has to face her fears. She experiences a night full of wonders. It also rains that night, and she gets wet. Despite all the hardship, she perseveres and stays there the whole night.

---

[21] This was Mura’s healing story in the section Cleansing the Family Karma on pp. 64-65.

At sunrise, she decides to stay a bit longer at this place and to enjoy it, instead of suffering. She has no watch with her, so she probably has lingered a bit too long. After a while, Ahamkara arrives, with a worried look on his face. He says: "Thank God you are still here!"

Then they walk back to the group together. It keeps on raining, also on the bus back to the airport. The morning after, just before they leave, Mura also receives her shamanic name from Ahamkara.

Mura's story is a proof of the local belief that those who respect Mount Belukha will overcome all challenges on the way and return transformed by their journey. For Mura, the journey is full of magic, color, and lessons about life and living in nature. She feels reborn and knows in her heart that she will return to the Altai one day.

DECEMBER 2024,
Luxwoude (NL)

I can hear the call of Mount Belukha. Has it not been calling me since I finally decided to walk my shamanic path for real in 2020? With every step, I am getting nearer to its skirts. I know I will be there one day, laying down on its bright green grass, smelling its beautiful flowers, drinking from its ice cold waters, and counting its infinite stars.

For the time being, I turn to YouTube for a virtual visit of Siberia. I am mesmerized, by the snow topped mountains, by the intensity of the colors, the emerald green forests, the blue lagoon lakes, the graceful horses... The air feels so crisp, as if you can feel it with your hands. And the emptiness, the feeling of forever. It is in these kinds of places where I feel how small I am in the vast ocean of life, and how abundant and gorgeous this planet we live on is.

I try to get a grip on how it feels to be there. I talk to those who have taken up this journey, like Mura and my classmate from the year training Mathilde. It is a journey of hardship, a journey of going to basics and of overcoming your comfort zone, they say. The further you walk towards Mount Belukha and the further you get from the inhabited world, the less people you run into along the way. Yet every person you encounter along the way, is in one way or another on a spiritual quest, seeking healing.

I ask Mathilde whether they have done rituals and healings along the route. I gather that the most important part of the journey is to become one with nature and to connect with it while being totally surrounded by it in its purest, untouched form.

It is about going to the river, like Germaine did, and hearing the tiny stone in the river talking to you, begging you to leave it there so that it can continue to bring healing there.

I already start dreaming about travelling to Siberia. It is now officially in my wish book. Just like joining Ahamkara's year training once was, meeting Mount Belukha is not a question of if, but rather a question of when.

What will I be seeking there? My roots, my ancestors from way back when, my past lives? I can feel the memories deep down: me racing through the steppes on a horseback. What else was I able to do back then? Was I the daughter of a shaman mother? Will my body recall some of the skills she taught me?

Mura tells me the veil is thin there. I love it when the veil is thin, just like these last days of the year. Feeling my pain, sitting with it, and releasing it. Drinking from the guidance of lucid dreams. Setting my intentions and wishes for the upcoming year.

I think back to the moments of travelling to the lands of my ancestors. Drinking from the waters of the rivers they shed their tears in, the tears of joy and sorrow. For me, the real magic lies each time in feeling and being conscious of these roots, traces, and cellular memories.

I think back to the first time I sat in a yurt, during my first shamanic training. The silence. The peace.

Let me sleep in a yurt, there in the heart of Asia, and receive the guidance of the wildest dreams while the only sound in the background is the fire crackling in the middle...

Dear life, take me to the Altai, when my wings are strong enough to fly and to carry my shamanic name.

SHAMANIC NAME

A **shamanic name** is a special name that symbolizes the change and transformation of a person, their connection with the spirit world and their mission on earth. It marks a turning point in a person's life. This name is not just a title but marks a deeper connection to the spirit world. It is a key to self-discovery as it helps to understand one's essence, the path of development, and the role they are meant to play.

A shamanic name can be received during a shamanic initiation or ritual and can be given either by an experienced shaman or by the spirits. It usually occurs during a ritual or ceremony when the person is in a trance or deep meditative state. Because a shamanic name carries spiritual power and responsibility, it should be given with respect and treated as a sacred gift.

Every shamanic name has its own purpose, meaning, and significance related to the qualities, abilities, and tasks of the person. It may be linked to an animal, a natural force, a plant or symbolize a certain quality of character or energy. It reflects something important about the person and the work they are meant to do.

Obtaining a shamanic name is a part of personal exploration. It helps you face your fears, see your strengths, and understand your potential. Such a name is not mandatory for all shamans or spiritual practitioners, but for some people it can be an important step in their spiritual growth and in helping others.

Ahamkara receives his shamanic name Ahamkara, meaning 'high consciousness', 'beyond the ego' in English, from his teacher. He does not start to use it right away. Sometimes it takes time to adopt and embrace a new name, yet a new name always means a new beginning, an opening of new doors. It represents a new life path.

Ahamkara has already been practicing for some time as a shaman-healer, but he was not feeling confident in teaching groups yet. He was even afraid and anxious of teaching. For him, this was the door that his shamanic name opened. After he really started using his shamanic name Ahamkara, he became the shaman-teacher and grew in his new role.

Mura knows what it means to make a fresh start by adopting a new name. Her birth name was Ruurdtje. She was named after her grandmother. She used to even wear her hair like hers and always felt that she was continuing the female line, also in terms of karma and the illnesses related to the lungs.

She adopted the name Mura in 2007, after the wedding ceremony Ahamkara performed for them as a couple to refresh their marriage bond. She only found out later on that this is actually the name of a river in Hungary, a land which she feels deeply connected with, through her past lives.

At the end of her journey to the Altai in 2013, Mura is initiated as a shaman by Ahamkara. She receives her shamanic name at the airport just before they leave. When Ahamkara goes in trance for her shamanic name, he receives the name

Umai. He asks Spirit three times, and the name is indeed 'Umai', Spirit confirms. Mura cannot believe she receives the name of such a powerful spirit. Ahamkara says: "Wait and see when you are ready to take up this name."

A shamanic name is connected to the spirit behind it, in Mura's case to Mother Umai. As the name also represents a new step in a person's development, you can only start using it when you can fully feel that you can carry this name and its meaning.

As much as Mura is amazed by her shamanic name Umai, the fact that it is such a powerful name means that she does not feel ready to use this name for years. She feels that it is a big responsibility to stand in service to Mother Earth.

Sometimes your new name and your new life phase needs time to be born. When I tell Mura that Umay is "just" a beautiful girl's name in Türkiye during our first meeting for this book, she comes one step closer to finally using it. Suddenly, her shamanic name feels a bit more "usual".

And as we talk about receiving our shamanic names from Ahamkara during the last lesson of our year training, I feel that she will finally start using it. That day arrives shortly after, on her 60th birthday in 2025. Mura is finally ready to rise up as the wise woman, Umai.

Germaine receives her shamanic name Eagleheart during her trip to Siberia in 2016, when she also receives her shamanic drum. Ahamkara receives the name Eagleheart as the spirits see that Germaine has a sharp sight and vision like the eagle and a very big heart for everything that is alive and needs to be nourished from the highest vibration.

Germaine falls in love with her name right away and starts using it in her healing work. She connects with the Eagle Spirit to fly towards the sun. At those moments, she feels deeply connected with the energy of the universe and to Tengri. It is one of the greatest feelings. Having sight and vision like an Eagle opens special doors for her: She starts from an eternal feeling of love and finds herself in a magical trance that she can steer. It is as if the Eagle takes her to a magical adventure in the spirit world.

FEBRUARY 2025,
Langezwaag (NL)

I go for my walk in the forest and experience a miracle. As I am looking for my birch wish tree with the intention of making wishes for the coming period of shamanic death and rebirth, I hear a knocking sound: 'Knock-knock. Knock-knock.'

It is as if a tree is calling me. The sound is so clear and strong that I turn back to find out which tree is calling me. I walk back and approach the birch tree to hear where the knocking comes from. It really seems like the sound is coming from within the tree, almost as if there is an animal inside, a living being for sure. I look at the tree from all sides – There are no holes, so it cannot be a bird nesting in the tree. Is it an animal moving up from under the ground? What could it possibly be? No idea!

My rational mind wants to explain this knock, whereas my soul wants to welcome it as a miracle, a beautiful call: My heart is singing with the thought that a tree that is talking to me.

I record a video of this moment as the knocking continues. Knock-knock. A heartbeat or is it the beating of a drum?

I am not able to translate the tree's message right away, so I admit this to the tree and say goodbye, and then: the knocking suddenly stops. Wow! So it was a miracle after all!

I continue my walk and find my wish tree and make my wishes. As I walk further, I discover another wish tree on my usual path for the first time. A larger wish tree where I can actually lean on with my spine and touch with my other two hands – the perfect tree for the wish ritual. Today is my lucky day!

I come home and feel the urge to check my Telegram, and there it is, the message I have been waiting for: my shamanic name.

I listen to Ahamkara's voice message: "I just dreamt about your shamanic name, and it came: Sky Mother. That's how I feel your shamanic name. It's connected with the future. That you help people bring the message, connect them with the future, with the sky."

And suddenly, it feels like everything falls into place – from my fascination with astrology all my life to the story of the birch tree that has been there from the start of my shamanic path. Connecting people to their future, helping to make their wishes come true, my company name Birth Wish.

And then the birch tree knocking and calling me today. I now feel that the tree was maybe even knocking at the same time as Ahamkara was drumming about my shamanic name. Such a blissful day.

Ahamkara also sends me a picture of a cloud in the sky, in the form of an angel, a mother with open arms. I love it! Sky Mother, reminding me of the tarot reading in 2014 opening my path to becoming a 'Mother of Mothers'.

I feel the power of this name, and I also feel I need to step up to it, to become more myself, the visionary, the fortuneteller. Does it even matter how? This is who I am, who I have always been. This is my soul, eternally calling me.

6

THE ETERNAL RIVER: TENGRI

There was a time when there was no earth, no sky, but only one vast ocean. One day, a White Light arose inside the ocean, from which a shining golden egg was formed. The god Tengri, the progenitor of the entire World, slept inside it. He slept for a very long time, millions and millions of years, and then one day he woke up. Tengri broke the shell of the egg and came out. From the upper part of the egg, Tengri created the Sky, and from the lower part, he made the Earth.

To prevent the Sky from falling to the Earth and the chaos reigning again, Tengri placed a staff (the Heavenly Stake) between them. Time and space 'spun' around it, and thus the World Order was established. The point where the staff enters the sky can be seen every night: This is the motionless **North Star**, which the Turks call 'the Heavenly Stake'.

Having separated Heaven and Earth, Tengri himself divided into a man and a woman to produce offspring. He called the female goddess Tengri Umai and settled her on top of Mount Sumeru, in the heavenly heights, where the milky lake Sutkol is located next to the Heavenly Mountain. The milk of Mother Umai is a star road, the **Milky Way**, which flows across the entire Sky and flows into the milky lake Sutkol.

Tengri's breath became the winds and the clouds; his voice became thunder; Tengri's right eye became the Sun, and his left eye became the Moon. And with the thunder and lightning during a thunderstorm, Tengri strikes evil spirits that prevent gods and people from living.

TENGRI: The Spirit of the Universe

Tengri is the spirit of the night sky, the spirit of the Universe, the high spirit. Tengri's energy is vertical, whereas the energies of Umai, Ulgen, and Erlik are horizontal. Tengri is the creator of the dream world and the material world. All that is around us is created by Tengri. In shamanism, Tengri is like God, the big Creator.

All souls that exist come from Tengri and go back to Tengri. We go back to Tengri every night when we sleep and after we die. We come to Tengri to rest and to start over again. Tengri gives us the opportunity to recover. Winter time and night time are the times of Tengri.

In the world of Tengri, there is actually no time. It is a timeless place. This is what you exactly feel at night: You do not feel time when you are sleeping. You are in the timeless ocean of Tengri.

The world of Tengri is a huge ocean of emptiness. Tengri embodies the highest energy. When we feel Tengri, we feel relaxed and safe. When we are connected to Tengri, we feel one with everything that exists, and we know that we are a part of that whole.

The biggest gift of Tengri energy is *consciousness*. It helps us to grow and to develop ourselves to our full potential in our life. Tengri gives us the opportunity to grow as a person. We connect with Tengri to raise to a higher frequency. One of the main tasks of human-beings is to raise their consciousness. When our consciousness grows, we can eventually reach the level of Tengri, but this is a long process that takes many lives. All souls follow this path and try to come back to Tengri.

CONSCIOUS LIVING & DREAMING

Ayi is a soul that we receive as a gift from Tengri. It is symbolized by the 'eye' on the shamanic map and represents **consciousness**, the ability to be aware of something. When your 'eye' is open, it means that you are conscious; when your 'eye' is closed, you are not conscious. (Be aware that this is not the same as the 'third eye' which refers to your ability to go to trance and to connect with your dream body!)

Conscious living lies in the heart of shamanic living. It is a way of life, a way of being, being with yourself, being present in life. Shamanic living is an art, an art worth learning and practicing, every single day.

Consciousness begins first with the self. You first need to become aware of yourself. When you are doing something, you have to feel yourself doing it. We are not only our bodies, but we are souls: *We are consciousness.* When you are aware of your consciousness, this means that you are observing yourself. And when you are aware of the fact that you are observing yourself, you *become* consciousness.

What do you have to do to be aware of yourself? Split your attention into two parts: one part is doing something, and the other is observing you doing something. The act of observing yourself makes you aware and conscious. Splitting your attention into two parts is not that easy though, as it requires more focus and energy. You need to train yourself to do this. Consider this as a training to strengthen your consciousness.

DECEMBER 2024,
Luxwoude (NL)

I listen to Ahamkara's lesson on Ayi, the eye, the consciousness. I find myself amazed once more by the realization that this shamanistic concept is actually embedded in the Turkish culture. Not only in the blue eye which is physically embedded in decorative and jewelry items to protect against the evil eye, but also in the concept of '*gönül gözü*', which refers to the soul's/heart's eye being open or closed. Loving my roots more and more as I dive deeper into shamanism.

And how about training my consciousness? I had ran across this concept of 'observing yourself while doing things' for the first time in Eckhart Tolle's book, *The Power of Now*[22] – a book that has definitely contributed to raising my presence in the moment. Back when I was reading Tolle's book, the concept seemed somewhat vague, but as I listen to Ahamkara explaining it as a daily practice of consciousness, I realize this might be one of the things I automatically do. I observe myself as long as I can remember, and I actually do not feel that this costs me extra energy.

This must also be a gift I was born with and never lost, like my first shaman teacher Petra (Altaiskaya Byelka) ever told me. Becoming aware of my gifts is what my shamanic path keeps on giving me. It feels time and again like I am walking way back home, to the origin of my own Ocean.

---

[22] Tolle, E. (2001) *The Power of Now: A Guide to Spiritual Enlightenment.* Hachette Collections.

CONNECTING WITH THE OCEAN OF TENGRI

The Ocean of Tengri, the eternal ocean where all our souls come from. Is this a place or a feeling? It is a place without borders, filled with infinite love, possibility, and wisdom. The place we long to as human-beings. Ironically, we feel this longing the strongest at times of suffering – When life on Earth becomes so unbearable that our souls long to escape to a different world, to a world we know the existence of deep down inside. In the darkest hours, we seek comfort in that ultimately soft and loving safe space. It is as though the harshness of our physical reality reminds us of the world of our soul, as a warm bath.

There is definitely one warm bath that we turn to and return to every single night – the sleep and the world of dreams. As Shakespeare so eloquently put it in *Macbeth:*

> *Me thought I heard a voice cry, "Sleep no more!*
> *Macbeth does murder sleep"—the innocent sleep,*
> *Sleep that knits up the raveled sleave of care,*
> *The death of each day's life, sore labor's bath,*
> *Balm of hurt minds, great nature's second course,*
> *Chief nourisher in life's feast.* [23]

---

[23] Translated to current English as: "I thought I heard a voice cry, 'Sleep no more! Macbeth murders sleep.' Innocent sleep. Sleep that smooths away all our fears and worries; that puts an end to each day; that eases the aches of the day's work; and soothes hurt minds. Sleep, the main and most nourishing course in the feast of life." Cited from https://www.litcharts.com/shakescleare/shakespeare-translations/macbeth/act-2-scene-2, accessed on 8 April 2025.

Sleep is "the death of each day's life", the "balm of hurt minds" in Shakespeare's beautiful words. Sleep recovers and regenerates us at all levels; sleep relaxes our body, repairs our cells, and helps us process the life experience we go through.

And sleep connects us with the world of dreams, the magical world through which we can tap into the infinite world of possibilities. It is in dreams that we can fly, with our wings wide open. It is in dreams that we connect with our ancestors and receive wisdom through words and symbols. The art is to open ourselves to this world, to the magical world of Tengri.

SEPTEMBER 2022,
Rotterdam (NL)

I wake up from a vivid dream that totally captures me. I am diving into a swimming pool. I swim through the bright blue waters of the pool. Then I see a shark approaching me. It opens its mouth, and I swim right into the shark's mouth. In total peace. I have no fear. I just surrender.

A week after this dream, I hear Ahamkara talk about night time dreaming during his weekly talk on YouTube and decide to contact him for the first time after our online meeting in April – this time for a dream interpretation. This rare dream about the shark has been lingering on in my psyche, so I am really curious about what he has to say about it.

I am grateful to receive a voice message from Ahamkara the next day. He interprets it as a

beautiful dream, symbolizing finding inner peace in a stressful situation that is unfolding around me.

Little do I know yet that just a few days later, we will finally be buying the village house I have been wishing for and will find myself in the middle of the stress of all the adjustments and arrangements that need to be made soon.

The shark dream is one of the many vivid dreams I see during this dreamful September. I am a big dreamer, but somehow these dreams feel significantly different. Could it be because of the spiritual book I am currently reading? It captivates me, and I feel that it is clearly expanding my consciousness. One night I even dream of myself flying through galaxies aligned in the color of the seven chakras. Wow!

And the dream with the number of our new house and the hint to the day we will receive the keys.[24] That dream will definitely go down in my personal dream history as one of my strongest predictive dreams!

SEPTEMBER 2024,
Luxwoude (NL)

I wake up in the morning from my dream where my father tells me that his mother, my last grandmother alive, has died. I turn on my phone right away and read the message my father has sent: "We have lost your grandmother."

Receiving this news first from Tengri... It is on days like this that I truly feel blessed, blessed

---

[24] The story about this dream was recounted in the section on Connecting with the Sky, on pp. 124-125.

for my connection to my dreams, to the world of Tengri, with all the wisdom and answers.

DECEMBER 2024,
Luxwoude (NL)

In Turkish, we have the term '*rüyaya yatmak*' which can be literally translated as lying down for a dream. Yet this is not as simple as it seems. It needs to be done consciously, with intention and prayers. This is what I intend to practice more often from now on.

I know the power of my dreams. I have had predictive dreams since my childhood. And the more I have these dreams, the better I get in reading the hidden symbols in these dreams. The next level for me is to ask explicitly for guidance and to read the messages I receive.

I experiment with lucid dreaming during this special period in the heart of winter, during the last days of the year when the veils are the thinnest. I ask, and I receive. What I receive is not always what I expect. I sink in the dream every morning, right after I wake up when the details are still fresh in my memory and take notes.

What I practice now with all the shamanic wisdom I have gained is to *feel the dream*, feel the energy and the presence of the people who appear. It feels enlightening. The messages are getting clearer.

It does not work this smoothly every day though. Maybe it is a matter of practicing. Or maybe as Ahamkara says: "Too much of anything is Erlik energy." Maybe asking for advice every night is also a bit too much after all!

I just need to relax, to keep on observing, reading, and trusting my dreams. I continue to consciously connect with the ocean of Tengri every night, now that I know even better how precious this time is.

Beloved darkness, beloved night sky, beloved Milky Way – the portal to the infinite world of Tengri. Remember to look up. Feel the eternity through the stars. Connect to your vastness and to your tiny being as a drop in this big ocean.

SEPTEMBER 2024,
Assen (NL)

I am in awe of Germaine as a person and as a healer. At the end of our first meeting, I cannot help but ask her whether she "sees anything about me".

"You need to connect with the stars" she says.

"I have always been interested in astrology" I reply, and I immediately think back to all those nights on the Turkish coast, of staring at the Milky Way in awe, of how I wished upon the stars to get pregnant for both of my children and how these wishes came true. I believe in the stars!

"Did you know that a falling star is the logo of my company Birth Wish?" I ask her enthusiastically. Then I remember a dream travel about the spirit of my business. The Milky Way, there it was again, reminding me I was on the right track. It is amazing, or as Germaine would

singingly say “It’s a kind of magic!”. The more I look for signs, the more synchronicities I find.

DECEMBER 2024,
Assen (NL)

“You need to connect with the stars” Germaine repeats.

“I have always been interested in astrology” I repeat.

“But I mean a deeper connection. Look at the stars; connect with them; work with them.” she explains. Note to self!

Then the healing begins. When Germaine says that my great-great-grandmother’s spirit has joined us, I recall immediately that she had the energy of Tengri when I had performed the shamanic ritual of connecting with the energies of our ancestors.

They say everyone is born with a mission, a life theme, which they carry in their name. I now also realize that her name Tevhide refers to the one and only God. I keep on being amazed by all the signs and magic of the universe, sprinkled around like little stars, patiently waiting to be noticed.

After the healing, Germaine says that she has put two stars on my eyes. I feel indeed that my energy has shifted. I now feel more of an urge to connect to Tengri.

No coincidence that I had already started to listen to Altai throat singing lately. Now I feel a new longing to learn this skill myself, to connect to these primal, sacred sounds coming from deep within.

I ask Ahamkara when we can expect to receive lessons on throat singing. Upon my request, he puts them on my online learning platform right away, and I start practicing with my son. My throat, which had been feeling blocked lately, already feels much more open after the first practice.

And I begin to wonder: Am I learning throat singing or am I actually just remembering it? We have always suspected that a part of my father's ancestors migrated from Central Asia to Anatolia. The records of our family tree do not go so far back to give us the answer for sure, but how about the cellular memory? How about the connection to horses in our family (name)? How about the visions I get of me riding swiftly on the back of a horse?

I listen to my latest discovery, the music band Altai Kai. This music... It touches me deep down, at a different place. I feel so humbled by this new connection with Tengri energy through music.

A week later I wake up after a beautiful dream. This time it is my grandmother, my mother's mother. She tells me about the stars and the universe. Hello synchronicity!

I turn my laptop on and check the newest lesson of our shamanic training: the very first lesson of the last block of our shamanic training, on the great spirit of Tengri. Hello synchronicity!

I share these synchronicities with Germaine. She is delighted to hear about the signs I share with her and to feel that the healing has brought me closer to Tengri. She also tells me she is really enjoying the jam I brought to her when I visited her for the healing, my grandma's quince jam

which I make every year to celebrate her death anniversary – the very grandma who appeared in my dream about the stars. Hello synchronicity!

The connection of it all blows my mind and fills me with joy. It feels like everything is falling to its place, like all the dots are connecting to each other.

The world of Tengri is different from the world of Umai, Ulgen, and Erlik. In the world of Tengri, images and sensations disappear. There is only the awareness that you are all that exists and all that exists is you. In the world of Tengri, there is an answer to all questions. You just need to ask in order to receive.

Shamanic Ritual: QUESTION TO TENGRI

1. *Find a question that is really important for you. The question must be clear.*
2. *Pronounce the question within you and feel the question as energy.*
3. *Rotate the body counterclockwise (feel the spiral) and send the question upwards to Tengri.*
4. *Relax the body in stillness while waiting for the answer.*
5. *Rotate the body clockwise (feel the spiral) and receive the response from Tengri. The answer comes in the form of energy.*
6. *Try to interpret the answer you receive in the form of images or messages. It may take a few minutes or a few days for you to clarify the answer for yourself.*

FEBRUARY 2025,
Luxwoude (NL)

I have already worked a few times with the Question to Tengri ritual. The very first time was when I asked about joining the organ massage course as I was doubting about the timing and the investment. And I was also scared, the kind of fear you feel before you embark on something new and important. The answer was clear back in 2023: a loud and clear 'Yes!'. And so I listened and am forever grateful that I took this step at that moment, instead of postponing it.

And here I am in 2025, on the verge of taking a step that I have been postponing for the last two years – buying a car for myself. I have been more anxious about the extra costs it will bring than the cost of the car itself. Finally, I decide to go for it after my father receives his inheritance from my grandmother and insists on giving some money to me as a gift.

I accept this gift and trust now that this new step will bring in new opportunities with it and not just new costs. Once I make this decision, the rest follows. I try out a car through the car dealer in our village. I trust the dealer and his advice, but somehow I just do not feel that this is my car. There are a few technical points (It is a second-hand car after all), but I also have an unexplainable gut feeling to postpone the decision to buy right away.

When we get back home from the car dealer, I use our pendulum, and it keeps on giving me doubtful answers to my questions about the car, like 'maybe' and 'try again'.

No useful answer comes forth from the pendulum, so I decide to perform the Question to Tengri ritual to find out if I should buy this particular car. The answer I hear right away is a 'No', but then the kids start curiously looking at me spiraling, and the ritual gets somewhat clouded.

I go to bed with the intention of receiving a clear message about the car in my night dream. Ask, and you shall receive: I dream of four crashed cars. This must be another loud and clear 'No' from Tengri!

I decide to get up – slightly earlier than usual – as I am wide awake from this dream. I go to the living room to repeat the Question to Tengri ritual. This time, in the silence of the morning hours. I hear one crystal clear answer from Tengri: NO! Me, finally: OK!

My intuition has always been strong, but my challenge in life has been rather one of following up on my intuition. Time and again, I have let my rational mind guide my choices and let my doubts overrule my choices. Result: Regret afterwards. And here I find myself again, doubting despite all these clear answers. "Doubt is ego" I recall Ahamkara saying.

I decide to call Germaine for support. I send her the link with the car and ask her to feel into it. I also tell her the story about my dream and the Question to Tengri rituals. She also does not feel like this car is right. She senses that there is something wrong with the brakes. She advises me to look further. We also call shortly, and then she invites me to answer the following question: "Will you listen to the advice from Tengri or to your rational mind?"

And I realize right there that this captures the heart of this story and all my stories of doubt and regret – now and in the past. This time around, I choose to listen to Tengri and decide to look further for other options.

The week after I try two other cars at another car dealer. The first one is a newer version of the car I tried first. This makes me realize immediately that the first car I tried was technically not ok indeed. I also discover that this specific brand and model is not the right car for me after I try a third car.

And with this car, I feel the 'Yes!' right away. For confirmation, I perform another Question to Tengri ritual when I leave the dealer and sit down in the park. The 'Yes!' comes right away, and at that moment the sun shines on my face before giving way to clouds a few seconds later.

This ray of light feels as a strong confirmation that my intuition is connected with the wisdom of Tengri, at all times – as long as I do not let my monkey mind interfere with the process! This time around, the Question to Tengri ritual, together with the guidance of Germaine, give me this precious insight, this ultimate pearl of wisdom to always trust and follow my intuition.

Sometimes, all we need is a clear answer and a helping hand to break age old patterns and to transform. At other times, we need stronger rituals to feel transformation in our bones – a shamanic death to mark the end of a period, so that we can begin a new one.

SHAMANIC DEATH

For shamanism, death in itself is a process of transformation, not a negative or scary experience. Death is a part of life. Each and every transformation processes we go through in life is actually a little death because every time something changes in our lives, we say goodbye to the 'old' thing, person, or behavior. When a baby starts to crawl, the baby who sits still dies. When a baby starts to walk, the baby who crawls dies.

With every new door opening, an old door closes. Something old has to die to make room for something new. Every time we separate with a partner or quit a job, we also die a bit because the part of us that was attached to that partner or job ceases to exist. Death is in this sense regeneration, as every death or ending leads to a new beginning.

Death is not that scary. It is like going to sleep. We love sleeping because it gives us the time to rest and recover, so that we can be ready and feel fresh for the new day that arrives. We are not afraid of going to sleep every night, yet while we are sleeping, we are actually disappearing from our waking life and are practically dead.

Our final death is the biggest transformation in our lifetime. Shamanism rests upon the belief of reincarnations and living many lives. Death is just the end of our current life, but after that we will live another life, just like we have lived many lives before in the past. We tend to be scared of our physical death because we do not remember our past lives, and we cannot foresee the end of our lives.

While we are alive, we can already get used to the idea of death. **Shamanic death** offers ways of getting acquainted with death spiritually through rituals. One of the intentions of shamanic death ceremonies is to learn more about death and to face the process of death, so that we can feel more at ease about dying. These ceremonies prepare us for death, which we experience during our lives in many different forms. When we feel ready for death, we can welcome it consciously as a part of our lives. Paradoxically, being conscious about death can help us to live fully and help us to fulfill our destiny for this lifetime.

Shamanic Death Ritual: The SIBERIAN SWEAT LODGE CEREMONY 'CHADIR'

I have been intrigued by shamanic death ceremonies since I have started reading on shamanism. It has been my wish and intention to experience shamanic death for some time now, as I want to feel it physically in my bones through ritual.

When my shamanic training classmate Mathilde informs me that Mura offers shamanic death rituals in the Siberian tradition, I know that this is the perfect opportunity to sign up for a shamanic death ceremony to mark the end of the shamanic year training with Ahamkara.

I also feel that my time for shamanic death has come. I see it as a door I should walk through

to be able to grow further on my shamanic path. The anticipation and excitement of this threshold grows in me in the month, weeks, and days leading up to it...

FEBRUARY 2025,
Orvelte (NL)

The big day has arrived: the shamanic death ceremony of the Siberian sweat lodge, *chadir*. The ceremony is led by two students of Ahamkara: Kees and Mura[25].

We are gathered as a group of six men and five women. It is always magical to see who ends up constituting your group, the souls that cross your journey, all walking their own path, yet present with their own unique energy to support your path at the same time.

Today, I feel grateful for the strong presence of male energy. After working on my female energy for years, I feel it is time for me to reembrace my male energy, so that I can fulfill my destiny and manifest my purpose with more power.

We start the day outside, around the fire. Kees and Mura explain how we will proceed, what we can expect, and how we can surrender to the transformative power of the sweat lodge. After the fire circle outside, we move inside for Mura's introduction into the world of the four big spirits

---

[25] During this ceremony, Mura had already began to use her shamanic name Umai. It was an honor to be a part of the first ceremony she led with her shamanic name. For clarity and consistency, I still refer to her as Mura during the account of this sweat lodge ceremony, as in the rest of this book.

of Siberian shamanism: Erlik, Umai, Ulgen, and Tengri.

By now, I have already learnt about the four big spirits during my two shamanic year trainings. Yet, I am amazed that the teachings in the spiritual domain never feel like mere repetition. Every shamanic teacher conveys this knowledge in another way, and every time I learn something new. My knowledge deepens every time, and I get to know the spirits better. I realize it is just like getting to know a person: It is an infinite well. And so it is today: I am happy to receive new insights and get a bit closer to each of these spirits through Mura's introduction.

Next, Mura invites us to dance with the energies of these four big spirits, with the help of music and the spirits of the animals. I recognize the elements of the online teachings of Ahamkara and now enjoy practicing this live with the group. And I love to see Mura in action. What a power woman!

We conclude with an intuitive massage with the energies of the four spirits. As I lay down to receive the massage, new insights begin to flow. While I receive messages about my ancestors, I see the sunrays shining through the window. Wow! I had not expected magic to show up so quickly today.

After this preparation round, Mura invites us to pick up a piece of wood and to bind a piece of rope for the emotional blockage we want to release and transform today during the sweat lodge ceremony. I had been contemplating on what I would like to receive insights on today, but not specifically on what I would like to let go and get rid of. When I do so now, one word in Dutch pops up in mind: *terughoudendheid*, Google translated as restraint, reserve, reticence.

Holding back my love, holding back my actions, holding back my words... Yes! This is it. I want to be more myself, without holding back. That is what I attach to the piece of wood and offer it to the fire in front of the sweat lodge. The fire will burn all the pieces of wood as we sit in the tent and sweat it all out.

I have a second offer to give to the fire: my old brown hair, the colored version before I had made the step to have my natural hair back as I was turning 42, which meant at that point that I would welcome my gray hair instead of hiding it under an artificial brown. This transformation was a big step then, towards embracing my age and my wisdom.

I had kept this piece of old hair because I was not ready to say goodbye to it right away, but it had been staying in a corner and even moved houses. In the end, this hair was not even my original brown hair – it was colored. And why did I actually ever start coloring my hair in the first place? Was that not the old me who was more receptive to societal expectations and did not embrace herself fully? Why was I still keeping this part of past me in my new house?

Shortly before the shamanic death ceremony, Mura had shared her story about offering her hair to the fire before her wedding blessing ceremony led by Ahamkara when she had also adopted the name Mura. I feel offering my hair will also be a nice symbolic step of leaving behind my "old me". Then I can make space for the new me and transition into using my shamanic name which I have received just a few days before the ceremony.

After preparing our offers, we go outside as Kees lights the fire under the stones of the lodge. As the stones are warming up, we place the blankets on the lodge one by one. Everyone is helping to build the lodge. It is teamwork!

The Siberian sweat lodge is a round tent. Just like a yurt, it is round like the womb, representing the beautiful Mother Earth Umai energy. This Siberian shamanic death ceremony has been designed by Ahamkara, and I definitely feel his presence today – both in spirit and through Kees and Mura. It also dawns on me that I am by now a part of his extended global spiritual family.

We each throw our offers to the fire outside the lodge and enter the lodge one by one, after being smudged by Mura. I actually look forward to the warmth of the fire on this beautiful winter day and suspect that I will even enjoy the intense heat of the sweat lodge.

The ceremony is divided into four parts, centered around the four big spirits: Erlik, Umai, Ulgen, and Tengri. The heat decreases as the ceremony progresses, and water is poured onto the fire with the last two spirits.

From the moment the ceremony begins, I feel gratitude for all the individuals who have gathered around the fire today. As the men in the group begin to make primal sounds, I am immediately thrown back to a very distant past – a distant past where communities used to gather around the fire for ceremonies, for warming up, for singing, or just for being together.

While I can hear and feel others in the group suffering through the heat of Erlik, for me personally Erlik feels like a walk in the park. I really enjoy the heat and feel that I am ready to let go of all that holds me back. As someone who enjoys radical transformation and change, Erlik feels like a trusted friend who has accompanied me throughout my life, and so he is here for me today, supporting me as always. I embrace his transformative fire.

After the Erlik ritual, I head out of the sweat lodge, to cool off but also to test whether it is actually the cold that gives me discomfort instead of the heat. The cold does not feel that cold at this point and is a welcome change of air. After drinking some water, I reenter the lodge for the Umai ritual.

I feel the Umai energy much stronger, so the harder work begins. Umai is here to tell me to embrace my personal power. This is what I am holding back – sharing my power, my gifts. This is where I need my first transformation.

Kees asks us to connect with our power animal and to feel if we need another power animal to support us. I thank the beautiful deer that has been helping me throughout the shamanic year training and welcome the horse who is ready to take me to newer heights. The Horse spirit, the spirit animal that guides our family, the animal that is anchored in our surname. The horse: my roots. What a blessing to receive this insight and support.

When I go outside after the Umai ritual, I feel the intensity of the heat that has built up in my body. I lay down directly on the ground without a towel underneath this time and let Mother Earth cool me off.

Just before we go back to the sweat lodge, it starts to rain. Mura is delighted to see that we are aligned with the energy of the Sky. I am excited and curious to connect next with the Ulgen energy. Since I have received my shamanic name Sky Mother, I have literally been in the clouds.

I am also hoping that the water pouring will lead to a cooler experience in the sweat lodge. To the contrary, I literally start burning with Ulgen! Ulgen is here to tell me it is not enough to own and share my personal power! It is now my task to rise up to my shamanic name!

As I fly with the Eagle spirit in the skies, I breathe in the vastness of possibility and abundance life provides us with. It is almost scary to feel that all that I dream of is possible: I CAN DO THIS! I CAN RECEIVE ALL THIS!

I dream a dream. I wish a wish. I give it to the hands of Ulgen. And I just trust that it will come true.

In the meantime, I am still burning. I ask Kees several times to pour some water on me. I am burning because I know the power of wishes, and yet I sometimes still fail to ask Ulgen's help in the process.

By now, I feel it in my whole body that I experience the fire getting warmer and warmer as it helps me to transform exactly where I need to heal. And for me, healing is needed in the greatness, in the creative power I own but fail to use. I notice with Ulgen that I am becoming more vocal, as if I find my voice again.

Come to me Ulgen! And please do not leave me until I become Sky Mother!

As I indulge in the new visions that appear in my dream world, I am deeply grateful for the new dreams, the new wishes, the new future that wants to unfold. As the Ulgen ritual comes to an end, I throw myself out of the sweat lodge again and let myself cool down on the earth. As I lay down, I look up to the mighty trees surrounding me and to the sky.

I crawl back to the sweat lodge for the last round. It is time for the Tengri ritual. This is the sacred energy I have been working with closely since December 2024. As I surrender to the silent space in the sweat lodge, I realize that my connection with Tengri has been there all along.

In the eternal silence, I meet my ancestors: my grandmas, great-grandmas, and the beautiful babies who died so soon in my family. I feel their presence. It is as if they are rejoicing my new energy. As I sit down with this strong female supportive energy though, it is like I am literally and figuratively fired up.

During this concluding Tengri ritual, I have to summon up my patience and perseverance to stay in the lodge and not to run outside into the cold instead. By now, I am sitting next to the 'door' of the lodge where it is supposed to be the coolest. Yet, it feels unbearably hot for me. 'Please, is the end near? I just cannot anymore!' my body is screaming.

This is the round where I really need to rely on my mental power to stay in the game, as it were. 'This is what I need to do to fulfill my destiny! I can do this.' I keep on telling myself. 'Stay conscious;

stay present; do not back away now!' I repeat to myself.

YESSSS! I DID IT!

What a magical experience! I have received new lessons, new insights, and new energy. I feel reborn, and I am ready to start anew.

I am grateful for the shamanic path which has led me here to this sweat lodge; grateful for the souls who have joined this journey today; and curiously looking forward to the light and power this shamanic death and rebirth will bring.

My first and foremost task: to bring this book to completion and to share it with the world.

7

CONCLUDING

With this book, we took you on a ride in the world of spirits through the lens of Siberian shamanism. By offering glimpses of our personal shamanic journeys, our intention has been to demonstrate that there is no fixed shamanic path. Every spiritual path is unique and led by the soul walking their path.

For Ahamkara, the shamanic path was a rather fast lane, even though he also had to overcome challenges along the way.

Ahamkara could see his life in front of him, in the palm of his hand when he was 23-years-old: He would work at a military factory; his career would proceed step-by-step from being an employee towards becoming the head of department. He would receive the apartment promised by his company, go to the beach for holidays once a year, and retire after thirty years.

When Ahamkara met his shaman teacher and saw his knowledge and energy though, he began to realize that his comfortable life actually made him sad. He weighed his options for some

time and he eventually decided to give up everything to go to Shaman Arzhan's mountain village in the Altai to study shamanism with him. This was his soul's calling.

From that moment on, his life completely changed. A whole new chapter opened with completely different energies, impressions, events, and experiences. He became aware of a completely different sense of freedom to live the way he wanted to. Ever since he has started to walk his shamanic path, he has never regretted his decision to become a shaman.

For Ahamkara, the experience of freedom is one of the deepest and most significant aspects of living a shamanic life. Shamanic practices, such as journeying and visioning, help him to break free from the constraints of everyday life and encounter the depths of his own being. They awaken a sense of connection with nature and the universe in him, allowing him to feel that he is a part of something greater, and unlimited beyond him. Shamanism gives him the freedom to be himself and opens the doors to a world of magic and spiritual harmony.

Ahamkara knows that there are many obstacles and difficulties awaiting a shaman, especially in terms of personal development and spiritual growth. There are several sources of support that help to overcome these challenges:

* Believe in your dream, in your shamanic path, and move on resolutely. If you cannot run, walk. If you cannot walk, crawl. If you cannot crawl, go and lie down in the direction of your goal. Take your steps, even if you do not know what the future will bring you.

* Take good care of yourself. A healthy body has a healthy mind and a healthy energy. In order to go into the unknown, you need strength, and a healthy body gives you more strength.

* Realize that overcoming challenges on your shamanic path helps you to build your strength. The more difficulties you have already overcome, the easier it is to overcome new ones. When you overcome small obstacles, you build up the strength to deal with big ones. The main thing is not to stop on the path of your development and to go where your soul tells you to go. Then all the obstacles have the potential to make you even stronger.

What has changed in Ahamkara's life since he has become a shaman?

First, there is much more responsibility in his life. As a shaman, his task is to help people. Shamans need to sincerely empathize with people to be able to help them solve problems and improve their life.

People come to him with a variety of problems: diseases of the internal organs, pain and discomfort in their muscles, fears, apathy, stress, problems in their relationships with their loved ones... Each story is unique.

When a shaman accepts the responsibility of helping someone, the spirits in turn give them the strength and energy they need in order to help them correctly. The spirits help the shaman, so that they can help their client towards a new life.

Ahamkara's life has become very busy over the years. He has contacts with more people, which also means that he has to process more new emotions, discoveries, impressions, and experiences. The story of each client is unique, and every time it feels like he is living their life together with them.

After practicing for more than twenty years and helping hundreds of people from Siberia, the Netherlands, Germany, Austria, Sweden, Belgium, and Switzerland, it sometimes feels like he has lived many different lives in many countries.

Embodying this special wisdom of the world leads people to treat him more respectfully as he has started perceiving much more than other people around him with this growing experience with diversity. He observes how everything works in the world and recognizes how people's actions lead to fears, illnesses, and problems in relationships. This helps him to understand what a person needs to change in their life in order to solve their problems.

As a shaman, he feels the clarity of his path, and he is confident that he can lead the life he wishes. At the same time, he also lives a completely ordinary life: He talks with his loved ones, goes to the store, the cinema, or the beach and reads books like everyone.

He does not feel the need to wear a shamanic costumes or to do 'special things' as a shaman. People already feel his energy and strength without all these ritualistic elements. The longer a shaman practices healing, the higher their vibration is and the brighter their life, even in terms of their daily routine.

Ahamkara is convinced that if you wish to do so, you can earn a good income with healing. Yet, even more importantly, people will also sincerely thank you for your work and help. The more Ahamkara helps people, the more happiness he feels. That is how his happiness grows every year, and it also multiplies through seeing his students grow on their own shamanic paths.

For Mura, the shamanic path has been one of patient and perseverant apprenticeship which has finally led step by step all the way towards offering her own shamanic year training as a teacher.

Mura's shamanic path has been clear and steady from the moment she embarked on it. She took her time to heal her own wounds and to learn from Ahamkara. Perhaps the most important lesson she learned from him, was how to overcome her own fears, the fears that kept her from moving forward and from growing further.

After setting up their own spiritual center Lumos, she began to walk further in her path as a teacher. Her visit to Siberia was a turning point. Not only did she experience a karmic healing of her ancestral wounds in the Altai, but she was also initiated as a shaman and received her shamanic name Umai. The experience of the nature and energies of the Altai left a lasting memory, and she carries the spirit of Siberia with her as she leads shamanic rituals and teaches her students. With lots of energy and enthusiasm, she continues to

share shamanic wisdom with her students and clients.

For Germaine, the shamanic path was more of an obligation than a calling. She had to learn the hard way. Even though she was born as a spiritually gifted baby, she had to go through shamanic disease twice before she finally chose to walk her shamanic path.

Germaine first needed shamanic healing and support for herself before she could open herself to shamanic wisdom. It was Ahamkara who saw the shamanic light in her and reassured her that she had psychic gifts, instead of a psychic illness.

Through her stays at Ahamkara's healing center in Siberia, she first healed her own wounds. Through the teachings of Ahamkara, she learned how to consciously be in contact with the spirits and not to be overwhelmed by them. Before Ahamkara, the reality and the dream world were mixed up for her, and now she can clearly separate these two worlds.

After accepting her gifts as a healer and medium, she has started to successfully help others. By now, she knows that she is a true *shamanka*[26] from deep within.

For her, shamanism is serious business. She is dedicated day and night to giving respect to all spirits, to helping all those who cross her path, and to praying for the well-being of the whole world.

---

[26] A female shaman

For me, the shamanic signs and hints have been scattered throughout my life, but it took me a shamanic disease to walk a long path of self-healing. And the path to shamanism followed, one small step at a time. I was the one who lied down if I could not crawl. I was the one who realized I could also walk while I kept on crawling. And nowadays I sometimes also run if I keep my eyes focused on flying high in the skies.

I healed with tiny baby steps, while I was wishing for a baby, until one day I realized I had taken up the task of healing ancestral wounds. It was then that the pain gave way to power.

I became a mother, through grief, through loss, through birth, but most of all by reading the signs and synchronicities. And then I decided to share what I learned with other women. As a doula, a mother of mothers, I hold space for women wishing to get pregnant, to be pregnant, and to birth consciously.

Once I started learning about shamanism, it was as if I got roots and wings at the same time. To me shamanism opens doors to discovering both the depths and the magic of human existence. Shamanism is a way of life that is grounded & raw and spiritual & eternal at the same time.

The shamanic journey for me is about seeing the beauty all around and about feeling beyond the five senses. It is about recognizing the signs and synchronicities that are present all around us in the material world and about feeling God through

these signs and messages, energetically and at a soul level.

My shamanic journey continues. The journey of self-healing is a lifelong process. The journey is full of surprises. Sometimes, it is slow and tiring to go through yet another swamp of Erlik. Sometimes, it is a beautiful walk through the forests of Umai. I am at my best while travelling in the skies of Ulgen, going after wishes, those of my own and others who ask for my support. And every night, I go to sleep in the arms of Tengri, feeling grateful for what the day has brought and looking forward to the dreams I receive.

With shamanic guidance, I feel peace and trust that all the questions will be answered; all the wishes will be fulfilled, as long as we ask the right questions and pay attention to the dreams, signs, and answers.

And I continue to learn and to walk my shamanic path to spread the wisdom – one healing story at a time.

This book has also been an important part of my journey. With this book, I have opened my heart and used my hands and my words to tell all the stories that have been shared and asked to be heard. It was a big step to tell my own story as well as the stories of my ancestors, of the women who have carried their grief and trauma in their hearts, in silence.

May all these stories heal our shared, collective pain.

We hope you enjoyed this journey through the world of Siberian shamanism, and that the shamanic teachings, wisdom, and tools we shared assist you both on the material and spiritual plane. Let us conclude this book with the basics rules of shamanic living as reminders to make the most of our precious *rivers of life.*

Shamanic Life Rules

1. ***Life is very short.*** Do not waste it on swearing, crying, profanity, or alcohol. Do good deeds; have children; rest and enjoy life's gifts!

2. ***Treat everyone with respect*** and do not put yourself above anyone else, even if you help someone. If selfishness or megalomania arises in you, it is better to come back down to earth, for nothing good will come out of it.

3. ***Never regret anything***: It is unnecessary. Everything happens by the will of the Spirits, and everything is happening for the best.

GRATITUDE

This book all started when Ahamkara said yes to my offer of documenting the core of the shamanic wisdom he has been generously sharing for years.

As I started interviewing him and asking him questions, the story started to shape up. Ahamkara has been present with his stories, ideas, support, trust, inspiration, and spirit throughout the way.

He has also been so generous to widen the story to include stories of his students. I am grateful for all the time, dedication, and effort Ahamkara, Mura, and Germaine have put into sharing their own life stories and holding space for me throughout this book journey. It was amazing to see the connecting lines between our paths and to receive heartfelt messages of trust and support during the whole writing and publishing process.

Our thanks and gratitude go also to all our ancestors and people who have joined and fed our healing path as teachers, family, friends, and soulmates.

May this book and its stories inspire more souls to discover themselves and the shamanic path.

WISH

SUMMER 2027,
Altai (RUS)

Ahamkara, Umai, Eagleheart, and Sky Mother are sitting around the campfire on the skirts of Mount Belukha. It is a soft summer evening in Siberia. The rest of the group is sleeping in their tents after a long day of walking.

Together we look back to the wild years of the River of Life on our beautiful Mother Earth. The wars have finally ended, and peace has returned. Many have died suffering, while others have discovered their spiritual gifts as human-beings in the midst of chaos.

As we look up to the skies, at the Milky Way in all its glory on this Altai night, we feel blessed to share and spread the shamanic wisdom and to be fulfilling our destinies in this eternal ocean.

Ahamkara then begins to drum, and we all begin to send our future wishes to the birch trees, for ourselves and the world. Whatever comes next, we know that we are all connected, in this life and beyond. And with this knowing, we soon drift into sleep in our sleeping bags, under a million stars, in the arms of Tengri.

ABOUT US

Shaman Ahamkara[27] is a practicing Siberian shaman and a researcher of the traditional knowledge of Siberia and the Altai. He uses shamanic diagnostic methods, breathing and trance techniques, and somatic bodywork for helping individuals to heal chronic health issues, (intergenerational) trauma and loss, to transform repeating life patterns, and to find direction and purpose in life. Ahamkara also offers online courses and educational programs on Siberian shamanism, energy work, and internal organs. His teachings are both for those with a shamanic calling and for those who seek personal development and healing. If the approach we presented in this book resonates with you, you can find Ahamkara's courses and offerings via:

Website https://ahamkara.org
Facebook https://www.facebook.com/ahamkara.eu
Instagram @ahamkara_shaman

[27] Photo: Evgeny Svetikov

Mura was born and raised in Franeker (the Netherlands). From a young age, she felt a deep attraction to the mystical, which later became the driving force of her life. In 2004, she rediscovered her ancient connection to shamanism, a bond that had long been present within her. After seven years of being a personal student of Ahamkara, she was initiated by him in the Altai in 2013 as a Siberian shaman and received her shamanic name **Umai**. She now offers shamanic trainings and ceremonies. For more information on her courses and offerings, please visit the website of Centrum Lumos: https://centrumlumos.nl.

Germaine was born in Assen (the Netherlands). Her life journey and spiritual gifts have led her to meet her great friend and teacher throughout many lifetimes: Ahamkara. Thanks to her work with him, the spirits, and her journeys to Siberia, she has embraced her gift as a healer and received the shamanic name **Eagleheart** in 2016. More information on Germaine's offerings can be found on https://germaineschoutens.nl.

Semin[28] was born and grew up in Istanbul (Türkiye) and moved to the Netherlands for pursing her PhD studies in Public Administration. After she accomplished her work in the academic field in 2013, she followed her heart's calling to start writing and to help women in their fertility, pregnancy, and birth journeys as a counselor and doula. In 2021, she embarked on her shamanic path by joining her first Siberian shamanic training, which brought her shortly after to Ahamkara and his teachings. She completed his internal organ massage and shamanic healer trainings and received her shamanic name **Sky Mother** in 2025. You can read more about her work and the types of support she offers via:

Website https://birthwish.nl
Instagram @birthwish.nl, @skymothering

[28] Photo: JLF Foto

www.ingramcontent.com/pod-product-compliance
Lightning Source LLC
LaVergne TN
LVHW091138080826
845145LV00008B/2190

* 9 7 8 9 0 8 3 6 6 5 5 0 4 *